LEADING

GOD'S PEOPLE

A HANDBOOK

ELDERS AND MINISTERS

Stewart Matthew Kenneth Scott

SAINT ANDREW PRESS • EDINBURGH

First published in 1986 by
SAINT ANDREW PRESS
121 George Street, Edinburgh EH2 4YN

This revised edition published in 1995.

British Library Cataloguing in Publication Data

A catalogue record for this book
is available from the British Library.

ISBN 0-7152-0706-7

Cover design and **internal layout** by Mark Blackadder.
Cover Photograph by Paul Turner.
Typesetting by Lesley A Taylor.
Printed by BPC Wheatons Ltd, Exeter.

CONTENTS

ABOUT
THE WRITERS

KENNETH SCOTT is senior lecturer in Social Sciences at Bell College of Technology, Hamilton. He is an elder in Viewfield Church, Stirling, where he has held several positions including Session Clerk and convenerships of education and pastoral committees. From 1983–89 he was Convener of the Church of Scotland's Eldership Working Party and is still involved in eldership training.

STEWART MATTHEW, until his death in 1991, was one of the Church of Scotland's National Adult Advisers and editor of its popular *Frontline* materials. He was minister of St Ninian's, Bellfield in Kilmarnock from 1969–79 and before that was a teacher of religious education at Swinton Comprehensive School in Yorkshire. His other books on eldership are *Caring for God's People* and *Session Matters* (both published by Saint Andrew Press). Throughout this book, under the heading 'Session Matters' various articles, written by Stewart, have been reprinted with the kind permission of *Life and Work*, the Church of Scotland's magazine, in which they first appeared.

KENNETH SCOTT

PREFACE
(to the 2nd edition)

It is with a mixture of gladness and regret that this preface introduces a second edition of *Leading God's People*. The joy comes from an awareness of the value which many elders have obtained from the first edition of the book and of the stimulus to action that many sessions have had from the ideas contained within it.

But the sadness arises from the knowledge that STEWART MATTHEW is no longer here to take the work forward. Stewart's vision and effort ensured a revived role for the eldership and a tremendous growth in eldership training. In particular, the network of elder trainers established within the Church of Scotland, the United Free Church and the Presbyterian Church of Southern Africa, is a tangible memorial to his pioneering work. In Stewart's own words, 'Think of the potential – elders leading congregations in a great nation-wide network! Enormous potential – requiring teamwork in Christ to release it'.

Thanks to SHEILAH STEVEN, National Adviser in Elder Training, for encouraging the revision of this work, and to all others who, either directly or indirectly, have contributed to it. My hope is that it will continue to promote Stewart's vision and to encourage elders everywhere to lead God's people ever more effectively.

KENNETH SCOTT
January 1995

STEWART MATTHEW

PREFACE
(to the original edition)

What is the job of an elder?

In our experience, having conducted many training programmes for elders, the usual answer to that question is 'to look after my district' – a commendable answer, but one far short of what this book attempts to set out.

What is the job of a Session?

It is interesting, and significant, that many elders find this a difficult question. Sometimes an answer is given like 'spiritual oversight of the congregation' – which sounds good, but what does it mean?

In *Leading God's People* we attempt to answer this crucial question.

In chapter 1 of the United Reformed Church's publication *Being An Elder* by S H Mayor it said: 'The Elder's job is not an academic exercise and it cannot be learned from a textbook.' We would agree. 'This book will not give you all the answers or make you into a "perfect elder"' – and neither will ours. But what we hope it will do is to help you grasp the importance and excitement of the leadership role of the collective body known in the Presbyterian form of Church government as 'the Session' or, as in the United Reformed Church, 'the Elders' Meeting'.

This book is about Session management – not in the sense of a dull primer for clerks telling them how to keep minutes – but in the sense of opening up the

---

**Dedication
of this Book**

~•~

'God
so loved
the world ....'

---

leadership role of the Session as we understand it for all elders. We believe that this leadership role, though readily agreed by elders in urban, rural and island settings, has yet to be understood by many, and that there is an urgent need for them to do so. We also believe that the principles outlined here are applicable in both large and small Sessions.

We do not attempt to trace the Biblical and historical origins of the eldership in great detail. That we leave to those more competent. But, having worked with hundreds of elders in many different places, and knowing the needs of today, we hope that *Leading God's People* will make a contribution towards realising the vast potential of today's eldership.

Using the book

We have consciously sub-titled this book 'A Handbook for Elders' because we hope that it will not only be read, but will be referred to and used by both individual elders and Session groups by reading each chapter in order and then using the exercises in chapter 7.

We hope you will find it helpful and stimulating to share the outcome of your thoughts and discussions with your fellow-elders in your own Sessions, and that it may provide a resource for those responsible for programming study-periods, retreats or conferences for elders.

We believe too that, with adaptation, this book will be of use to other Christian groups to whom the privilege of leadership is given.

It dawned on me with a sudden jolt that real prayer, Christian prayer, inevitably drives a person, sooner or later, out of his or her little group of Christian friends and across the barriers between social, racial and economic strata to find the wholeness, the closeness of Christ in that involvement with the lives of his lost and groping children whoever and wherever they may be.'

KEITH MILLER

INTRODUCTION

It is hoped that this book will be of use to the elders of various Presbyterian denominations. In the main, the terminology of the Church of Scotland is used. For those of other traditions the following word of explanation is given:

CHURCH OF SCOTLAND	IRISH PRESBYTERIAN	PRESBYTERIAN CHURCH OF WALES	UNITED REFORMED CHURCH
Kirk Session *or* Session	= Kirk Session	= Elders' Meeting	= Elders' Meeting
Session Clerk	= Clerk of Session	= Church Secretary	= Church Secretary
Congregational Board	= Congregational Committee	= Properties Committee	= Elders' Meeting *or* special sub-committee
Presbytery	= Presbytery	= Presbytery	= District Council
Elder's District	= Elder's District	= Elder's District	= Elder's Group

NB: *In the United Reformed Church, the Elders' Meeting is subject to the Church Meeting in a way that is not so in the other traditions.*

BASELINE THINKING

About life

We believe that life is about relationships. It is made good, bad or indifferent largely by the quality of our relationships. We hazard the guess that we could be very rich and yet live an unhappy, unfulfilled life if our relationships with husband/wife, family, neighbours, workmates are not good.

WE ARE MADE BY LOVE FOR LOVING.

We dare to say that life in a primitive setting, without many of the things we consider to be essentials, can be good if relationships with family and the wider community are good.

As Christians we believe that we are made by a God of love for loving.

With the Bible (indeed with other faiths, God-centred or not) we believe that humankind (collectively and individually) live in 'sin'. What this means has been expressed in many ways. For us the word 'separation' is helpful. Humankind lives in a state of separation.

WE LIVE IN A STATE OF SEPARATION.

The Bible sees this state of separation in 3 ways:

1 *Separation from one another*

Any newspaper shows, column after column, the separation between East and West, North and South; one nation and another; one class and another; one political party and another; one person and another. Every newspaper is full of physical violence and the violence of neglect. Most of us will have first-hand experience of this state of separation in the very streets where we live and in our own family circles.

2 *Inner separation*

Do you talk to yourself? Do you have different voices in you that pull you in separate directions? Do you ever feel separated somehow from the happiness, fulfilment, freedom you long for? Can you say with Paul that the good you want to do, you don't do, while the wrong you don't want to do, you often do?

JESUS IS ABOUT
AT-ONE-MENT.

3 *Separation from God*

CHRISTIANITY IS ABOUT
COMMUNITY THROUGH
JESUS CHRIST.

Saint Augustine wrote these chord-striking words: 'You have made us Lord in your own image and our hearts are restless until they find their rest in you.'

Life is about relationships. It is not meant to be lived in this three-fold state of destructive separation which spoils happiness.

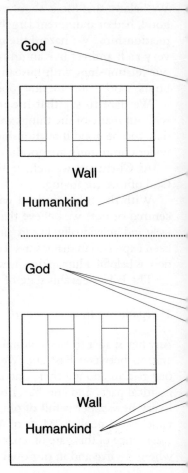

About the Gospel

We believe that the Christian good news is about *shalom*. In Luke 2:14 the message proclaimed through the figure of the angel is that the coming of Jesus is about *shalom* – peace – a word which can be looked at in three particular ways:

* peace with one another;
* inner peace for the individual;
* peace between us and God.

Jesus is about peace, atonement, at-one-ment. Jesus is about the overcoming of our three-fold separation. And so we believe that Christianity is about community through Jesus Christ.

About the Church

We believe that the purpose and the ministry of the Christian Church originates from Jesus and his ministry which can be understood in the light of the purpose God gave to the people, Israel.

Israel's calling is expressed in Genesis 12:1-3, where it talks about Abraham going forth in faith and obedience to a land he was promised by God. Great promises are made to him and to the people whose father he was to become. The end of verse 2 says that he, and they, are to be a blessing. Through them (verse 3) all the families of the earth are to be able to find blessing.

How?

Israel was meant to live a lifestyle of faith and obedience that reflected the love of God for all His creation, so that those who lived outside their faith would have the opportunity to share the blessing of their faith.

Amos 4:1 – the society women of Amos' day, back in the eighth century BC, were condemned for telling their husbands to bring home a bottle of wine after work while the heads of the poor in their society were being crushed into the dust. Life could not be so organised in Israel. Gross inequality and injustice are not a true reflection of God.

Deuteronomy 10:18-19 – as God had cared for Israel while a stranger in the land of Egypt, so Israel must look after any stranger in its midst. The stranger, surprised at this, is encouraged to enquire into Israel's faith, and receives the opportunity to find the blessing of that faith for himself. The whole passage (vv 12-22) is worth studying.

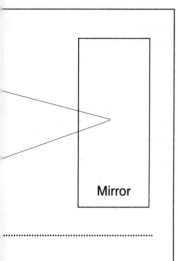

Mirror

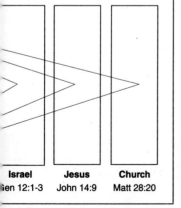

Israel	Jesus	Church
Gen 12:1-3	John 14:9	Matt 28:20

◄ This diagram (left) seeks, through the analogy of a wall and a mirror, to explain Israel's calling. In this life we cannot see God directly with our eyes. If a mirror were put across the end of the wall we could see the reflection of the One who stands behind the 'wall'.

The Old Testament story is about Israel's failure to provide that mirror – to live up to its calling – reflecting God's love and offering the blessing of faith.

Consider Jesus in the light of the diagram (see previous page). John 14:9 – 'He who has seen me has seen the Father'. The New Testament writers try to express the wonder and the meaning of Jesus in various ways, as Christians have done in every generation. Most would agree, whatever else they might want to say, that we see in Jesus – in what he said and did – the God in whom we believe.

Jesus, in his own person, fulfilled the calling of Israel and brought about his Church to continue God's ministry of reconciliation and blessing.

We are meant so to live in our congregations, caring for one another and for those outside our faith, that on both counts they are attracted to enquire into the reasons for our lifestyle and so get the chance to find the blessing that is ours through Jesus Christ.

We are the 'Our Father' people, who gather around the Table of the Lord to be equipped for our ministry in the world. Our ministry to each other and to the world is a shared ministry.

WE ARE THE 'OUR FATHER' PEOPLE, WHO GATHER AROUND THE TABLE OF THE LORD TO BE EQUIPPED FOR OUR MINISTRY IN THE WORLD. OUR MINISTRY TO EACH OTHER AND TO THE WORLD IS A SHARED MINISTRY.

We are a people with a mission

Have a look at Mark 1:16–17, Matthew 5:14–16, Acts 1:8, 1 Peter 2:5,9–10:

> *This is one of the most vital things the Church needs to discover at the present time; that the power of a visible and collective community will far surpass the sum of the community as individuals.*
>
> Michael Harper

We are sure that Michael Harper does not mean to diminish the importance of a Christian's individual witness in a political party, union or boardroom, school staffroom or shop counter, or over the fence with neighbours. What he is stressing, however, is the importance of our congregations as visible communities. It is often less easy to dismiss the witness of a community than that of an individual.

THE DOWN-PIECE OF THE
MAIN CHRISTIAN SYMBOL
CAN BE SAID TO REPRESENT
THE VITALLY IMPORTANT
PERSONAL RELATIONSHIP
EACH OF US CAN HAVE WITH
GOD.

FOR THOSE OF US WHO
ARE CHRISTIANS, THE
CROSS-PIECE IS ALSO
ESSENTIAL, SYMBOLISING
OUR RELATIONSHIP WITH
OTHERS.

Be that as it may, we would wish to emphasise the importance of Christian community. In our culture, Christianity, and religion in general, has come to be considered a very individual and private matter.

The down-piece of the main Christian symbol can be said to represent the vitally important personal relationship each of us can have with God. For those of us who are Christians, the cross-piece is also essential, symbolising our relationship with others. In Jesus' teaching the two are so bound together. Consider Matthew 5:23-24.

The Christian life is meant to be a corporate experience.
John Sherill

Our fellowship is part of that mission

Now, have a look at John 5:12, Hebrews 10:24-25, Ephesians 4:32, 1 Peter 4:8.

Our churches must be real communities .... They have largely been preaching points and activity generators. Community has had little place .... Every Christian church should be a community which the world may look at as a pilot plant.
Francis Schaeffer

Francis Schaeffer feels that real Christian community has been neglected in our congregations. While much of their activity is good, such as organisations that care for the elderly and young, it has to be admitted that much of what goes on might be described as 'pastiming'. Badminton clubs, secular drama groups and the like, do have a value. But they rarely provide community in the New Testament sense of Christians enjoying a depth of sharing which permits us to rejoice when one of us has cause to rejoice and to share the pain when one of us is in difficulties. Have a look at Romans 12:15 which follows the call so to care, even for those who persecute us.

We feel Schaeffer's idea of a congregation providing a model of how, in Jesus, the whole of society could be, fits our wall/mirror analogy well (see pp 2-3) and presents us with a vision and a challenge.

Contributing to the failure to grasp the corporate (at-one-ment) nature of the Church has been the choice, by the translators of the Authorised Version of the Bible, of the word 'church' rather than the word 'congregation' for the original Greek word *ekklesia*. The word *ekklesia* was used in New Testament times of societies and decision-making bodies whose members met regularly together. In Acts 7:38 there is mention of the congregation of Israel 'in the wilderness'.

> *The Christian image of the word 'church' often suggests something static and inactive .... The Old Testament background gives it a different flavour. The 'church in the wilderness' was something dynamic, a people on the move, migrating together to a glorious destination.*
>
> Michael Griffiths
> *Cinderella with Amnesia*

MINISTRY BELONGS TO THE WHOLE PEOPLE OF GOD.

Our shared ministry

Let's underline this fundamental point:

> *It is a spiritual tragedy of incalculable proportions that we have come to restrict 'ministry' to what 'the minister' does.*
>
> D F Wright, *Eldership*

That may sound a bit extreme, but we thoroughly agree with it and fear for the future of the Church unless it is grasped.

The distinction between the ministers, the elders and the ordinary members developed early in the history of the Church.

It is not our purpose to explain this development of clericalism, as it is called, nor to apportion blame for the deep-rooted holding on to it. We simply wish to state yet again that the ministry as we have tried to explain it, was the purpose of Israel as a whole. It was what Jesus fulfilled in his own person and brought the Christian Church into being to continue.

Those we call 'ministers' – rightly or wrongly – have a key function, but 'the ministry' belongs to the whole people of God. Congregations can be lined up more or less on one side or other of the semi-colon in the following quotation:

> *The laymen are not there to help the minister run the church; the minister is there to help the laymen be the Church.*

(Source unknown)

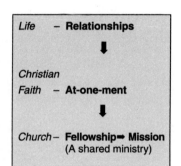

Life   – **Relationships**

⬇

Christian
Faith   – **At-one-ment**

⬇

Church– **Fellowship➡ Mission**
            (A shared ministry)

ALL CHURCH–PEOPLE MAY
NOT BE CHRISTIANS, BUT
ALL CHRISTIANS ARE
CHURCH–PEOPLE.

We would wish to re-write the second half to read: 'the minister is there to help his fellow lay-people be the Church.' The terms 'laymen' and 'laity' refer to the whole people of God to which the 'minister' belongs. *Shared ministry develops from this understanding.*

All church-people may not be Christians, but all Christians are church-people: part of Christian Fellowship and Mission. Our thinking can be summarised ◀ (see table, left).

About the eldership

Old Testament

Elders were important to the life of Israel. We read in Numbers 11:16 – 'The Lord said to Moses, assemble seventy respected men who are recognised as leaders of the people ....' Some three thousand years ago it would have been unlikely to have included women in such a choice. However, regardless of gender, we notice the emphasis on the choice being made on the basis of recognised leadership qualities which in our age and society are certainly not held by the male gender exclusively!

Verse 17: 'I will take some of the spirit I have given you and give it to them ....'

We note the importance of God's inspiration.

'Then they can help you bear the responsibility for these people and you will not have to bear it alone.' The responsibility referred to cannot be understood purely in terms of Moses and the seventy ministering exclusively to God's People, because as Israel they had a shared ministry to each other and to the outsider. We see the responsibility of Moses and the seventy in terms of leadership.

Verse 29: 'I wish that the Lord would give his spirit to all his people and make *all of them* shout like prophets.'

A prophet was someone who spoke forth (not fore-told) God's word as he/she understood it.

Moses and his elders were meant to lead, equip, enable Israel to fulfil its God-given calling.

New Testament

By the time of Jesus every synagogue had its elders who were the real leaders of the Jewish communities. Some elders had a national role as members of the Jewish Sanhedrin or Council which met in Jerusalem.

Jesus gathered around him a group of people, his disciples (learners), whom he trained to be the leaders of his Church. They became known as apostles (those sent out on a mission).

The apostles, including Paul, established Christian communities or associations, often based on households which became congregations as the Church rapidly grew.

Many forms of leadership developed as people exercised various God-given gifts: gifts of prophecy, instruction, admonition, care of the poor, administration.

It is interesting to contrast Numbers 11:29 with Ephesians 4:11-12, where it speaks about God's gifts being given and people being appointed in the Christian communities:

> *'Some to be apostles, others to be prophets, others to be evangelists, others to be pastors and teachers .... '*

For what purpose?
> *' ... to prepare ... '*

Who?
> *' ... all God's people ... '*

For what?
> *' ... for the work of Christian service.'*

That is, for our shared ministry of witnessing to the Gospel of the grace of God (Acts 20-24).

In the New Testament we see a great variety of leadership models and clear evidence of team ministries, as we can see in 1 Thessalonians 1:1; Romans 12:3-8; 1 Corinthians 12:27-31.

> *We find about eighty personal names in the authentic letters of Paul of whom it can be said that they toiled for the community in one way or another, as teachers (male or female), leaders (male or female) of house communities, as evangelists and prophets, as deacons or whatever, either in local communities or as itinerant preachers of the Gospel.*
>
> E Schillebeeckx
> *The Church with a Human Face*

Certain titles began to be used and came to have a long history in the good ordering of the Church:

- *Elders* (from the New Testament Greek *presbyteroi*);
- *Overseers* or *Bishops* (*episcopoi*);
- and *Deacons* (*diaconoi*).

(for Biblical references see p 19)

The fact that elders appeared in the early Church, often coupled with the Apostles, is not surprising given the long tradition of the elder in Jewish society; but what was exactly meant by the term is unclear, as is the relationship between the titles mentioned above.

In Acts 6 we read about Stephen and others being appointed to wait at the table so that the Apostles can get on with the ministry of the word. Stephen and the others are often thought of as deacons with care of the poor high on their agenda. But we read of Stephen's miracles and signs (v 8) and of his efforts at evangelism and teaching, which has made some wonder whether he and the others had in fact not been made elders.

It is not easy to distinguish elder from bishop as in Titus 1:5-9. Both titles may have been used of the same position, or the latter may have been the chairman or leader of the team of elders of a Church community.

Presbyteroi and *episcopoi* may have been in the early Church more akin to what in our Reformed traditions we would call 'ministers'.

In 1 Timothy 5:17 a distinction appears to be made between different kinds of elder.

In Philippians 1:1 both bishops and deacons are mentioned. Clearly they were complementary roles in the leadership of the shared ministry of God's Church.

Professor T F Torrance in *Eldership in the Reformed Church* (Handsel Press) writes about today's elders:

> *The nature of the office elders hold and the kind of functions they perform bear a close resemblance to the office and function of the deacon described in the Pastoral Epistles and early Church documents. There we learn that deacons fulfilled an important assistant ministry in the Church in association with bishops and presbyters, and had particularly to do with the ministry of the divine mercy and with seeking the fruit of it in the life and mission of the community ....*

We are not attempting here to trace in any great detail the origins, Biblical and historical, of the eldership. On page 19, along with Biblical references, we offer some recommended reading for those who wish to pursue this matter further.

What is clear to us is that:

> ... *attempts to recreate the exact form of Church order that was current in the New Testament period run into insuperable difficulties. In particular it is quite clear that there was no single uniform pattern in operation in the early Christian congregations ....*

and that:

> ... *if we take the New Testament seriously we should not rest content with one-person ministry. It is impossible to justify the solitary position we give to the minister. Every congregation reflected in the New Testament was looked after by a variety and plurality of ministers.*
>
> D F Wright, *Eldership*

We would agree that:

> ... *if we are to follow the Biblical pattern it is right that a local congregation should have a body of dedicated men and women, carefully chosen and properly commissioned, to look after the welfare of the church and its members in every way possible.*
>
> Stephen Mayor
> *Being an Elder in the United Reformed Church*

IF WE ARE TO FOLLOW THE BIBLICAL PATTERN IT IS RIGHT THAT A LOCAL CONGREGATION SHOULD HAVE A BODY OF DEDICATED MEN AND WOMEN, CAREFULLY CHOSEN AND PROPERLY COMMISSIONED, TO LOOK AFTER THE WELFARE OF THE CHURCH AND ITS MEMBERS IN EVERY WAY POSSIBLE.
Stephen Mayor
Being an Elder in the United Reformed Church

In Acts 20:17-38 we are shown the kind of spirit that should be in the leadership body. Luke tells us about Paul calling together the leaders of the church in Ephesus. He shares with them his life and ministry, including his concern regarding the future. He feels that he will not see them again and charges them to look after their congregation and its witness and the proclamation of the Gospel. Before he leaves they all pray together and their affection for each other is openly expressed.

Reformation

At the Reformation the office of the elder was given a key role with ministers and elders working in part-nership in the leadership of congregations.

The elders' role, therefore, is not to be limited to district work, to pastoral concern for the members of a congregation. Their work will include this, but their main task is the important overall task of leadership – of together leading the lifestyle of their congregation in terms of its fellowship (its ministry to each other) and its mission (its ministry to the world).

The Session, the collective name for the elders of a congregation, is concerned with the lifestyle of the congregation – its fellowship life and its outreach – in the area it is called to serve.

The collective role of the elders acting together as Session is greater than the sum of the individual elders in their pastoral work.

THE COLLECTIVE ROLE OF THE ELDERS ACTING TOGETHER AS SESSION IS GREATER THAN THE SUM OF THE INDIVIDUAL ELDERS IN THEIR PASTORAL WORK.

Ordination

In our Reformed tradition:

> *... because of the great importance of elders, they are ordained. Ordination here, as in the case of ministers, implies the solemn recognition and ratification by the Church of a divine call.*
>
> S H Mayor
> *Being an Elder ...*

Ordination has been described as:

> *... an action by God and the community (Church) by which the ordained are strengthened by the Spirit for*

their task and are upheld by the acknowledgement and prayers of the congregation.

'Baptism, Eucharist and Ministry'
Faith and Order Paper No III (1982)
World Council of Churches

Selection of new elders in the *Church of Scotland* is by the Session, which may or may not choose to involve the congregation in the selection procedure. We have more to say about this on page 57-58.

In the *Presbyterian Church of Wales* elders are selected by the whole congregation present on the chosen election day.

In the *United Reformed Church* selection is also by the congregation, a fact underlined by vows taken by the congregation at the ordination service for elders.

Ordination is for life

AN ELDER IS APPOINTED TO A PARTICULAR SESSION TO EXERCISE, ALONG WITH FELLOW-ELDERS, THE VITAL JOB OF THE LEADERSHIP OF THE CONGREGATION.

Such a step is not to be taken, nor the invitation given, lightly or thoughtlessly, but with reverence and dedication, since the vows to be taken are akin to the vows of marriage, and are just as long-term in their intention. Anything less would, in our opinion, diminish the office.

An elder is, however, only 'active' while carrying out duties with a particular Session.

An elder can resign from his/her Session, for example when leaving the area, and retain the status as long as the resignation is accepted. Entry into another Session is not automatic, but by invitation.

'Divorce' is possible. An elder can seek release from office. An elder can also be removed from office.

An elder is appointed to a particular Session to exercise, along with fellow-elders, the vital job of the leadership of the congregation.

VOWS OF ORDINATION

Following their own individual statements about their denomination's understanding of the faith, the purpose of the Church and its form of government, the various churches require the following vows to be taken by those being ordained:

United Reformed Church in the UK

Do you confess again your faith in one God, Father, Son and Holy Spirit?

In dependence on God's grace do you re-affirm your trust in Jesus Christ as Saviour and Lord, and your promise to follow him and to seek to do and to bear his will all the days of your life?

Do you believe that the Word of God in the Old and New Testaments discerned under the guidance of the Holy Spirit is the supreme authority for the faith and conduct of all God's people?

Do you accept the office of elder in this congregation and promise to perform its duties being your helper God?

Presbyterian Church of Wales

Are you prepared to accept the call extended to you by accepting the position of elder in our Connexion, and do you promise to work faithfully with your minister and fellow-elders to promote/facilitate the work of the Church.

Do you promise, through the grace of God, to do your best to live a sober, just and Godly life, remembering at all times the honour of the position to which you have been called so that you do not at any time bring dishonour upon the Fair Church of God?

Church of Scotland

Do you believe the fundamental doctrines of the Christian faith; do you promise to seek the unity and peace of this Church; to uphold its doctrine, worship, government and discipline; and to take your due part in the administration of its affairs?

United Presbyterian Church of the USA

Following vows regarding trust in Christ, acceptance of the Bible, the place of the Confessions of that denomination, these other vows are added:

Will you be a friend among your comrades in ministry, working with them, subject to the ordering of God's word and Spirit?

Will you govern the way you live, by following the Lord Jesus Christ, loving neighbours, and working for the reconciliation of the world?

Will you seek to serve the people with energy, intelligence, imagination and love?

Will you be a faithful elder, watching over the people, providing for their worship and instruction?

Will you share in the government and discipline, serving in the courts of the Church, and in your ministry, will you try to show the love and justice of Jesus Christ?

THE ELDERSHIP IN THE REFORMED CHURCH

In the Church of Scotland's *Common Order* (1994) the minister is encouraged to exhort the congregation at the ordination of elders to receive the elders into their homes and *share with them the task of the Church.*

In the United Reformed Church the minister asks the people to stand and says to them:

> *I now call on you, the members of this congregation, to dedicate yourselves anew to Christ and to the task of ministry which he lays on us all, and to promise your support to the new elders in their work.*

Three questions are then put, the response being *'We do':*

Do you confess again your faith in Jesus Christ as Saviour and Lord?

Do you seek to fulfil together your common calling to the glory of the one God, Father, Son and Holy Spirit?

Do you promise to give these elders, whom you have elected to share in the pastoral oversight of this church, your support and encouragement in the Lord?

What has been written about the eldership in the Reformed tradition

Most of the quotations below refer to 'he' rather than 'she'. They were written prior to the decision (in the case of the Church of Scotland in 1966) to admit women to the eldership. No insult is intended by the present authors.

'The eldership is a spiritual function as is the ministry' – so declared the Church of Scotland's *Second Book of Discipline*, indicating that in the Presbyterian form of Church government, ministers and elders are closely associated.

One of the characteristics of the ecclesiastical organisations which had developed over the centuries was clericalism and the Reformers sought to combat and remove clericalism by involving the laity in the life and work of the Church in new ways. One of the ways was through the eldership which involved representatives of the Church in its government and work alongside those who ministered the Word and the Sacraments. Calvin taught eventually that 'elders and deacons' should be associated with the pastors and teachers (or doctors) of the Church in the pastoral care of the Church members and in the government of the Church. He believed that they had a crucial role to play in the exercise of discipline or pastoral care in the Church, as the Genevan Ecclesiastical Ordinances of 1841 stated:

THE ELDERSHIP IN THE REFORMED CHURCH (cont'd)

Their office is to take care of the life of everyone amiably, to admonish those whom they see weakening, or leading a disorderly life, and, where it may be advisable, to bear report to the company which will be deputed to apply brotherly correction.

(A) (see book references on pp 18-19)

The following quotations from the Church of Scotland's Practice and Procedure **(B)** bring out the common recognition of the joint, or corporate, role of the Session and the very common interpretation of pastoral concern in terms of discipline.

The office of the elders is severally and conjunctly to watch over the flock committed to their charge both publicly and privately, that no corruption of religion or manners enter therein. **(B)**

As pastors and doctors should be diligent in sowing the seed of the Word, so the elders should be careful in seeking the fruit of it in the people. **(B)**

Maintenance

It would be hard to find fault with this, but alongside it there usually appears a marked legalism:

It appertains to them to assist the minister in examining them that come to the Lord's Table. **(B)**

In 1648 it seems that the General Assembly of the Church of Scotland instituted elders' districts

… as one of the remedies for profaneness. **(B)**

The first care of the Kirk Session should be for the welfare of the congregation. **(C)**

This sounds more positive, but it is defined very much in terms of maintaining the *status quo.*

To the Kirk Session are assigned such essential duties as regulating the hours of public worship, appointing special services and the time and place for the observance of the Lord's Supper, seeing that all children connected with the congregation are baptised without needless delay and, wherever possible, in the House of God, and caring for the religious training of the young. **(C)**

It is sometimes said that the duties of the eldership are three-fold: to attend meetings of Session, to look after an elder's district, to assist with the distribution of Bread and Wine on a Communion Sunday, and in all things affecting the welfare of the congregation, to be an example to others. **(D)**

Often, in our judgement, little content is put into what are described as essential duties.

The tradition and probably still the best way of establishing this contact (ie with church members) is for the elder to take round the cards for communicants at least twice a year. **(C)**

THE ELDERSHIP IN THE REFORMED CHURCH (cont'd)

The same passage suggests that:

> ... *causes of illness or misfortune may at the same time be discovered which had not been made known to the minister.* (**C**)

We would not consider two visits *per annum,* linked to the delivering of the Communion card, to constitute real pastoral concern, nor are we happy with the pastoral role of the elder made so inferior to that of the minister. We are encouraged to read, even in the above passage:

> ... *there are suffering and lonely people who will welcome a short prayer from a visiting elder in the intervals – often of necessity somewhat long intervals – between the minister's pastoral visits.* (**C**)

That is certainly an improvement on:

> *It is no part of the elder's official duty to pray with the sick.* (**B**)

In previous writings about the eldership some very useful and sound things are said about the example an elder should be. We would want to endorse this, although we would also counsel caution against the danger of double standards.

> *The eldership is a spiritual office and only a man who has something of the Spirit of God in him can fulfil it in any way. Unspiritual men in the Session lower the spiritual temperature of the Church and destroy its power. That is why the devotional life of the elder is of supreme importance.* (**D**)

The devotional life of *every member* of the Church is similarly very important.

Leadership

Publications by G F Barbour (**C**) and W C Macdonald (**D**) mentioned on pp 18-19 do refer to the leadership role of the Session, but, for us, a real turning point came with a little Iona Community pamphlet by G D Wilkie (**E**) (see pp 18-19). Speaking about the elder in the Church of Scotland, he says:

> *At the formative period of the office of elder, the Church was a recognised institution in a stable society – an institution which continued the same from generation to generation. In such a situation the Kirk Session could easily become the Committee which dealt with the routine matters of Church life.* (**E**)

Who could disagree with the writer that this has now changed!

> *No longer is the Church popularly accepted as a necessary institution. It cannot even assume a continuation of its present position and everywhere it must fight again for the acceptance of what it stands for ... everywhere it must be on the offensive penetrating and permeating the new society in which we find ourselves with the truths of the Christian faith.*
>
> *If this is to be accomplished, a new understanding of the position and function of the elder is essential. No longer will it do for the Kirk Session to be the Committee which keeps the age-old*

THE ELDERSHIP IN THE REFORMED CHURCH (cont'd)

wheels of Church life turning. It must become a body of trained and experienced men directing and leading the mission of the congregation. (**E**)

The above publication is no longer available, but its clarion call was echoed in a later publication by D F Anderson (**F**).

Spiritual insight of the members: Christian adult education: these are two of the main functions of the Kirk Session today. I would add a third: the urgent need of the Church today is for more positive leadership from the Kirk Session .... [It] is not meant merely to keep things ticking over – doing maintenance work – but to act as a policy-making body for the whole church. (**F**)

In the 1970s the Church of Scotland's influential Committee of Forty made various recommendations regarding the development of the leadership role.

The most profound value of the eldership today lies in its potential. (**G**)

The more recent Church of Scotland *Frontline* materials have contributed towards the liberation of this potential:

In the Presbyterian system the Kirk Session is where the buck stops. The labours of the theologians, the charismatic leaders, the church committees, the General Assembly, the British and World Council of Churches are as nothing if the Kirk Sessions do not fulfil their tasks. (**H**)

A useful publication from the United Reformed Church says:

... a local Church should have a body of dedicated men and women, carefully chosen and properly commissioned. (**I**)

Another publication by D F Wright states:

The elders and ordained ministers are best regarded as the team ministry of the congregation. (**J**)

If that means, as we think it means, that the Session, which includes the minister, is the leadership team of the congregation's ministry, then wholeheartedly we agree. The Session is the 'team of the team'.

Materials referred to regarding eldership

(**A**) *Training Courses for Elders* (Presbyterian Church of Ireland).
(**B**) J T Cox: *Practice and Procedure in the Church of Scotland* (from sixth edition, 1976).
(**C**) G F Balfour: *The Elder and his Work* (Saint Andrew Press, 1977 – no longer available).
(**D**) *The Elder: Character and Duties*, W C Macdonald (Stirling Tract Enterprise, 1958; Saint Andrew Press 1982).
(**E**) G D Wilkie: *The Eldership Today* (Iona Community, 1958).
(**F**) D F Anderson: *The Elder in the Church Today* (Saint Andrew Press, 1968 – no longer available).

Materials referred to regarding eldership (cont'd)

(G) *Parishes – Elders – Assembly: Committee of Forty Report to General Assembly* (1976).
(H) I Strachan: 'Thinking About ... Training for Elders', *Frontline A3* (Church of Scotland Department of Education, 1981).
(I) S Mayor: *Being an Elder – in the United Reformed Church Today* (Church and Life Department, United Reformed Church).
(J) D F Wright: *Eldership* (Rutherford House, 1984 – no longer available).

Biblical references to elders, bishops/overseers and deacons

ELDERS: Old Testament
- *Among other peoples*
Genesis 50:7 – Egyptians
Numbers 22:7 – Moabites

- *In Israel (local and national)*
Exodus 3:16; 12:21; 18:12; 24:1
Leviticus 4:15
Numbers 11:16-20
Deuteronomy 19:12; 21:1-9, 18-31; 25:5-7; 27:1; 29:10; 31:23
Joshua 7:6; Judges 8:16; Ruth 4:2
1 Samuel 15:30; 16:4
2 Samuel 5:3; 17:4, 15
1 Kings 8:3; 21:11
2 Kings 6:32; 10:1
2 Chronicles 5:4; Ezra 10:14

Psalms 107:32; Proverbs 37:23
Lamentations 1:19; 4:16; 5:12
Ezekiel 8:1; 20:1; Joel 1:14

New Testament
- *Jewish Elders*
Matthew 16:21; 21:23; 26:57; 27:1, 20, 41; 28:12
Mark 8:31; 15:1; Luke 9:22; 22:66
Acts 4:5, 8, 23; 6:12; 24:1; 25:15

- *Christian Elders*
Acts 11:30; 14:23; 15:4, 23; 16:4; 20:17-38
1 Timothy 5:1, 17, 19
Titus 1:5-9; James 5:14-15; 1 Peter 5:1-5
2 John 1; 3 John 1
Revelation 4:4-11; 5:1-14; 7:9-17

BISHOPS/OVERSEERS
Acts 1:20; 20:28
Philippians 1:1; 1 Timothy 3:16
Titus 1:7-9; 1 Peter 2:25

DEACONS
Philippians 1:1; 1 Timothy 3:8, 10, 12

For further study:

Edward Schillebeeckx: *The Church with a Human Face* (SCM, 1985).
T F Torrance: *Eldership in the Reformed Church* (Handsel Press, 1984).
Church of Scotland Panel on Doctrine: 'The Origins of the Eldership' in the *Blue Book* (Church of Scotland, 1964), pp 753-757.
Church of Scotland Panel on Doctrine: 'Ministry: An Interim Report' in the *Blue Book* (Church of Scotland, 1985), pp 143-161.

SESSION MATTERS

SESSION MATTERS

When new blood comes in

Before going to my first charge I had read everything I could lay my hands on about the previous life of the congregation. Continuity is important. I remember, however, making a silly mistake. Indeed, I remember making many silly mistakes. This particular one related to the congregational magazine.

A new editor was required, and being interested in Church journalism I assumed the task. I began a new-look, new-format magazine and, while retaining the same title for the magazine, brought out my first edition as Volume 1, number 1!

Because the new minister did not live the congregation's past, it can be, for him or her, as if it never existed. A new elder can fall into the same trap.

We owe the past much, but we can need help to understand it and so be helped to understand the present and to move forwards effectively.

Is it too idealistic to believe that a Session should be willing and able to explain to its new minister or new ruling elders what, as the leadership team of the congregation, it has been trying to achieve in the years prior to their arrival? Should it not be able to articulate its strengths and weaknesses, its hopes and dreams for the future?

Should the Session not also be open to the new members' hopes and dreams; to their understanding of the purpose of a congregation and the nature of its shared ministry, including the role of the Session (which includes the minister)? 'We never did it that way before … ' can be a right enthusiasm crusher. As the prophet said: 'Where there is no vision, the people perish.'

A Session requires times of reassessment when it asks itself some very basic questions about its work. Experience, it is often said, is our teacher. But it is not that simple. Without reassessment, the same mistake may be perpetrated for years and the same blind points go unnoticed.

An annual stewardship theme is a useful policy to have. By stewardship I don't just mean the financial aspect of the congregation, but rather the whole lifestyle of the congregation. The theme can be the response to the basic question: 'What is God calling us to concentrate on in particular in our part of His vineyard?' I wonder how many Sessions regularly pause along the way to ask such a question and to enable them to move forward.

Someone once wrote: 'We are pilgrims, travellers, adventurers and all the while we must be travelling on.'

LEADERSHIP

Leadership means enabling people to achieve what they want, or require, to achieve. What we want to achieve are called our goals.

A Christian congregation is no different from any other group in this respect. It requires leadership and it has goals. Whatever else a local church may be about, it is reasonable to suggest that it should at least be about:

1 *Believing:* grasping something of the wonder of Jesus Christ.
2 *Learning:* following Him by becoming 'disciples' (learners or students).
3 *Sharing:* being part of a fellowship of mutual support and love with each other and with God.
4 *Proclaiming:* reaching out to others with the good news of the Gospel and becoming 'apostles' (*ie* people with a message to share).

The Session ought to be about enabling the local congregation to be the People of God in the place where they are.

In buildings like this church (see right) the Christian Church seeks to live as *outposts of the Kingdom of God.*

A true Church is an outpost of the Kingdom of God, placed in a particular spot in the world to bear witness to the Lordship of Christ.

A Church is a mission, living by the foolishness of God in a world that sometimes hates it, sometimes is

Our baseline thinking can now be summarised thus:

Life   – **Relationships**

↓

Christian
Faith   – **At-one-ment**

↓

Church   – **Fellowship➡ Mission**
                    (A shared ministry)

↓

Session – **Leadership**

indifferent, and sometimes seeks to take it captive.
    Any Church that does not recognise the basic purpose for its existence is in jeopardy of its life.

Otto Webber

We find the understanding of a local congregation as an 'outpost' of the Kingdom of God an exciting one and a most meaningful one.

Settlers, far from their home, establish a colony, an outpost of their way of life in a hostile environment. They require leadership, self-discipline, loyalty. To survive they must care for each other.

We must regard the local congregation as having a certain real primacy among the various units into which we may think of the church as being divided. That body of neighbours who share in the same loaf and the same cup, who form the visible company in which the Word is preached, and who, being neighbours, are able in the context of actual personal meeting to build one another up in the faith and to correct one another in love and to wait upon the Lord for his guidance, has a strong claim to be regarded as the primary unit of Christian fellowship.

Lesslie Newbigin

There is no place for in-fighting, for anything which saps the strength of God's settlers and gives ammunition to the enemy. Not only must they survive, they must also make ground.

The business of the Church is not to attend to its own life. It has Christ to attend to that. He is its nourisher. It must not concentrate on stoking its own fires, sustaining a comfortable temperature of givings and attendances and activities for itself .... If it would find life, it must lose it. It must concentrate on the object of God's love — the wide world.

Ian Fraser

A LOCAL CHURCH SHOULD BE ABOUT:

BELIEVING: IN THE WONDER OF JESUS CHRIST

LEARNING: BY BECOMING A DISCIPLE OR 'LEARNER' OF HIM

SHARING: BEING PART OF A FELLOWSHIP OF LOVE WITH EACH OTHER AND WITH GOD

PROCLAIMING: SPREADING THE GOSPEL'S GOOD NEWS

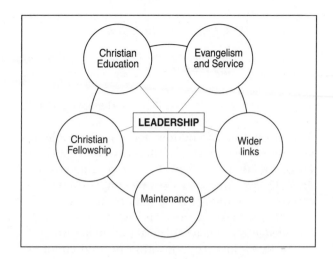

The Constitution of the Church of Scotland defines a congregation as '*a company of persons (members, adherents and their children) associated in a particular locality for Christian worship, instruction, fellowship and work.*

It is the task of the Session to provide the soil for developing 'discipleship' and encouraging 'apostleship'. We believe that the local congregation should be a Christian resource centre where people are equipped and supported to live, enjoy and learn to share their faith with each other and the wider community.

This is the goal towards which the leadership of the Session should be aiming: an exciting, participatory and meaningful congregational lifestyle. It can only be achieved by elders who are themselves serious 'disciples' and 'apostles'.

The diagram at the top of this page outlines areas in which Session leadership is necessary to achieve such a congregational lifestyle.

Christian education

Go, then, to all peoples everywhere and make them my disciples ... and teach them to obey everything I have commanded you.

Matthew 28:19-20

The instruction of children and young people is a very traditional concern of the Session – rightly so. However, education should not be confined to children. That is a mistake too many congregations have made for too long. It is now more important than ever that Christian men and women should be knowledgeable and articulate about their faith.

CHRISTIAN LIVING AT ITS BEST IS ALWAYS EXPLORATION IN THE COMPANY OF OTHERS.

And yet Christian education beyond children's Sunday School level is still infrequent or not seriously offered at all. It has been said that Jesus played with children and taught adults – whereas the Church teaches children and plays with adults. A look at the normal organisations of many a congregation and the programmes that they offer seems to confirm this all too often.

Adult education is necessary both for the enlightenment of members and to help people to develop those skills necessary for the work which Christians have to do in the Church and in the world. The Sunday sermon alone is a limited, and in some ways an ineffective, means of attaining these ends.

A wide range and variety of opportunities to cater for various needs is required. The chart on the opposite page summarises some of them.

★ ★ ★

The Church of Scotland's Education Department has a slogan. In its ecumenical version it reads:

'Every local congregation –
A Christian Resource Centre –
The Frontline in Christian Education.'

... Elders need to know and understand the life of the contemporary Church.

FORMS OF ADULT EDUCATION

INFORMAL LEARNING

- Organise resources for learning (books, materials, networks of people) geared to the likely learning needs, and make access easy.
- Promote informal conversation by making chances for it to happen and providing an environment full of things to talk about (*eg* exhibitions).
- Engage in learning by stealth, using what people do like to do to encourage a need to learn (*eg* banner-making).
- Make sure everything you do in the church, from business to worship, shows that learning pays off.
- Make it a priority to train people who can make informal learning happen.

SHORT-TERM GROUPS

some then identify issues as needs they wish to pursue further.

Make your main formal learning to be limited term, and geared to specific needs or skills (eg bereavement groups).

LONGER-TERM GROUPS

some then wish to set them in a systematic framework.

Don't stop offering things for the interest-motivated groupies. Be glad you've got them. But build bridges from other activities into the curriculum. Don't let longer-term groups 'congeal' (*eg* a 2 year course on basic belief).

OPPORTUNITIES BEYOND THE LOCAL CHURCH

some may discover particular roles or needs to go beyond this level.

people enter at any level

Also build bridges to learning opportunities beyond the local church, whether Church programmes or secular ones (*eg* distance learning, national courses).

The more Scottish version reads:

'Every Parish Church –
A Christian Resource Centre
Led by its Kirk Session –
The Frontline in Christian Education.'

The members of a local congregation are called to
be 'stewards of the Gospel' (1 Corinthians 4:1).

The lifestyle, therefore, of a Christian congregation should be full of opportunities to 'grow', 'learn',
'mature', 'become' (key New Testament words).

Sessions that understand this:

- provide training for elders;
- include study periods in Session meetings;
- have annual retreats or conferences;
- encourage house groups in districts;
- set up an education committee.

Where better to start than in the Session itself. If the
Session is afraid of learning, then the congregation
is likely to be deprived.

Fear of ignorance and revealing one's ignorance
are great inhibiting factors. We should not, however, discount ourselves, nor our God who, with our
co-operation, can remove mountains of ignorance.

Christian fellowship

But if we live in the light – just as he is in the light – then we have fellowship with one another.

1 John 1:7

What is your congregation like? Your answer might be put in observable terms: the number who attend services; the range of organisations; the age-sex span of members; the amount of church activity.

It might better be defined in terms of *quality* and *growth*. The great danger for the Church is that it has become a 'monument', rather than a 'movement'. It stands still, rather than developing and maturing as any healthy organism must do if it is to survive.

It is part of the Session's leadership task to ensure such development and growth. As many people as possible need to be meaningfully involved in the work and witness of the local congregation.

Worship

Worship is probably still the main focus of attention for the majority of church members. The minister has a particular concern for the conduct of worship, but there are many instances where the involvement of elders is both appropriate and valuable.

The main example of this is the Communion service. Legally this is not a Session act and the use of elders to serve the elements may owe more to administrative convenience than to theology. However it is an instance of participation in worship which could be extended to other occasions.

The shortage of ministers is a factor here and any elders with gifts in this sphere are often used in multi-congregation charges.

With the agreement and co-operation of the minister, even in normal situations members of the Session could help to plan and lead worship, and could participate, say, in the reading of the Scripture lessons and in the leading of some of the prayers.

A Session could consider various developments regarding worship – at different times of the day, on Sundays and on other days in the sanctuary, and in other settings, using a variety of formats.

House groups

As well as the large-scale Sunday service, the house group can provide an important, helpful and complementary opportunity for members to worship together, to relate to each other, to engage in study, discussion and caring.

It is important that house groups are developed as a natural part of the life of the congregation. In our belief they are not a mere extra, or something peripheral, but belong at the heart of the life of the congregation. They are very much a matter for the Session.

Social activities

Social activities can make an important contribution to the building up of congregations and the development of Christian fellowship. Congregational picnics, parties and social events can be fruitful vehicles for people to come together, to learn more about each other, and to enjoy themselves.

The existing pattern of Church organisations falls into the habit of catering for specific age or sex categories: for example, children, women, mothers, teenagers. Such limiting barriers could be reduced and more all-age events might be attempted.

Pastoral care

Be happy with those who are happy, weep with those who weep. Romans 12:15

Because of the strong tradition that every elder should

Model for Action

'Welcome Duty' is the name some congregations give to 'door duty' because its real purpose is to communicate to all the worshippers that we are glad to see them in God's house. A welcoming face, even a warm handshake, help to set the right atmosphere for Christian worship.

When handing over hymnbooks and service bulletins elders are encouraged to greet people by name or to ask a person's name. Being known by name is important.

Visitors can be identified and may be escorted to a seat and introduced to a neighbour. They are invited to sign the visitors' book as they leave (allowing a follow-up if they live in the area). They are also invited to after-service refreshments.

look after a district, the task of pastoral care is one of which the Session might be expected to be highly aware. But pastoral concern is not to be confused with the delivery of communion cards!

> *To each elder there is normally assigned a district for the oversight of which he/she is responsible. Each elder should assist the minister in the care of the sick, the aged and the needy, and in encouraging those outside the fellowship of the Church.*
>
> The Office of the Elder in the Church of Scotland
> (Church of Scotland Panel on Doctrine)

THE AIM OF PROPER PASTORAL CARE IS TO MAKE REAL PERSONAL CONTACT WITH PEOPLE. THIS MEANS SHARING BOTH THE JOYS AND THE SORROWS, THE SUCCESSES AND THE DIFFICULTIES OF OUR FELLOW CHRISTIANS IN THE INTIMACY OF THEIR OWN HOMES. IT MEANS PROVIDING LOVING SUPPORT AND A SENSE OF BELONGING.

The above certainly calls for far more than the delivering of communion cards. The aim of proper pastoral care is to make real personal contact with people. This means sharing both the joys and the sorrows, the successes and the difficulties of our fellow Christians in the intimacy of their own homes. It means providing loving support and a sense of belonging.

Sessions need to create a pattern of congregational life and a set of attitudes that can support members with personal problems:

- bereavement and other loss situations;
- illness and hospitalisation;
- family troubles; emotional distress;
- money problems; redundancy/unemployment;
- doubt and loss of faith.

Thus all types of individuals within the congregation need to be looked after and to receive care and attention:

- the housebound; those in hospitals and homes;
- the bereaved; those out of work;
- all members within one family;
- the lapsed; the active and committed.

Yet pastoral concern on the part of the Session is often exercised at a purely superficial level. This may be partly because full pastoral care is seen as the job of the minister, rather than as part of the commitment of elders, and indeed of every Christian (see the 'Care Visiting Scheme' in Appendix 1, page 125).

No one individual can hope to look after the personal needs of a whole congregation satisfactorily. And so the Session must play its part in the shared ministry of mutual love and care.

This caring encompasses members of the Session themselves, including the minister whose position is a demanding and sometimes lonely one. Where should ministers, and indeed all elders, be able to turn in times of trouble if not to fellow elders?

If we are not taking real care of each other it is unlikely that we are developing a spirit of real caring in the congregation, members for members, let alone members for non-members.

Evangelism and service

You are the chosen race, the King's priests, the holy nation, God's own people, chosen to proclaim the wonderful acts of God, who called you from the darkness into his own marvellous light.　　　1 Peter 2:9

What is an evangelist? We would say that it is any Christian who shares his/her good faith with others and who proclaims the good news of the Gospel to those outside the Church.

Emil Brunner once wrote: '*A church lives by mission, as a fire lives by burning: no burning, no fire; no mission, no church.*' Mission is such a central part of the message of the Gospel that it is impossible for a congregation to justify fully its existence without evidence of some outreach to others.

The institutional Church can often be so sadly lacking in missionary zeal.

FELLOWSHIP
EDUCATION
WORSHIP
OUTREACH

CAN ALL BE GENERATED
IN A HOUSEGROUP

SESSION MATTERS

SESSION MATTERS

In at the deep end

Should an elder pray when he visits a house in his district?

If beneath this there lies the question of whether an elder should *ever* pray in the homes of his/her district, I would believe the answer is a clear affirmative.

Christians should be able to pray together. It's hard to disagree with that, so why should those who have been ordained as the spiritual leaders of a congregation not be permitted to pray with their fellow members in their districts? Indeed they should be willing and able to do so.

I don't think we should, however, make a law out of a means of Grace. There may be times when it is not appropriate to lead a prayer on a visit. Faced by a non-member husband, who resents his wife's involvement in the congregation, might not be the time. On the other hand, it might.

Experience tells me that there are far more people who welcome being led in prayer than I would have believed. We must remember, however, that this is not something we, to satisfy *our* needs and self-expectations, do to others regardless of their needs and wishes.

If we haven't done this before, what's the best way to start?

Perhaps in your district you have a housebound member no longer able to take his/her place in the pews, or to hear the Scriptures read at a service of Worship. Remind the person he is still very much part of God's family. Ask if he would like you to read a passage of Scripture with him: perhaps Psalm 23. Few will decline the invitation. After the reading, quietly, simply, sincerely lead a prayer thanking God for the faith offered to us in the Psalm; for our belonging to the Church; and for his blessing on your fellow-member and yourself. You may find that, following this, your visit begins. If, however, you leave then, you will have made a pastoral visit, having pointed your fellow-Christian to his God.

Perhaps a new family has come into your district. Before you leave on your first visit, suggest that together you ask for God's blessing on their new home. You might read Jesus' teaching, at the end of the Sermon on the Mount, about building a house on rock rather than sand. Ask for God's blessing on this new home, giving thanks for the privilege you have of being part of it, and seeking God's help to ensure that its foundations are firmly based.

I don't know what the 'best way to begin' is. I do know that if we are to learn to swim we must get into the water and we must get more than our toes wet!

Mission is closely linked to Christian education and fellowship. We should want to argue that the lack of evangelism reflects a lack of education and fellowship within Sessions and congregations. As Christians, we cannot share what we have not ourselves experienced.

The Session needs to be conscious of, and alert to, occasions when mission can be promoted at a number of levels.

On a personal level, individual Christians need more help and support than they normally get to become evangelists. By praying together, studying the Bible together, talking about the faith together, we can gain the knowledge and confidence required to be the missionary Christians we so often fail to be.

Sometimes, evangelism may take the form of a structured and continuing programme. For example, some means can be developed of identifying and approaching newcomers to the area, perhaps through church members who live in the same street. Or circumstances might be appropriate for setting up a mission station in the area not accessible to the church building, as in a housing scheme or remote countryside.

Sometimes, evangelism might involve a major initiative on the part of the Session. An area visitation in which every household is approached is a popular form of this. Or it might be some kind of outreach project designed to communicate the Christian message to a specific group, say young people, or people without work, or to shoppers, or to holidaymakers.

Service

Sharing in mission also involves giving through service. The Church, to be true to the Gospel, must live for others, and giving is a basic commitment of both the individual Christian and the corporate congregation:

Here's an idea ...!

Family focus

Run a course of 4-5 meetings entitled 'Your Child and You'. Invite *all* parents, including lone parents. Use good speakers – doctors, psychiatrists or teachers. Choose Christians whose faith is related to what they are saying.

Into the community

What about open-air? Have an Easter March or Pentecost celebration outside. Is there a place where people regularly gather: a square, beach? Train your young people to direct street theatre or have Songs of Praise outside on a Summer evening. If you have a church garden, use it for worship sometimes. Open-air Easter-dawn services, followed by breakfast, are common. Note 'Make Way' material by Graham Kendrick specially designed for open-air work.

Festival time

Make the most of the Christian Festivals. Despite the decline in UK church attendance, 30% of the population will be in church at Easter and 40% at Christmas. In rural communities, Harvest Festivals are when the community comes to church, and many places are seeing potential of Mothering Sunday as a day to celebrate God's gift of family.

- Plan early.
- Involve a range of people.
- Ensure worship is for *all* ages; easily understood by visitors; focussed on the central truths of the Gospel.
- Be imaginative and bold.
- Use professional publicity: *eg* posters, invitation cards, simple literature.
- Contact the community in the 10 days before the Festival.
- Prepare welcome cards for visitors at worship to fill in for follow-up.
- Prepare members of the congregation to visit or offer hospitality to visitors in the following 2 weeks.

At Christmas

- Prepare special services through Advent for different groups (*eg* Sunday School, Choir, Youth Fellowship).
- 'Think visitor' in all communication. Avoid everything being for children.
- Invite visitors to complete welcome cards if they wish a visit after the New Year.
- Take to the streets with carols! Offer a message rather than money.

'Developing the Missionary Parish', from *Here's an Idea: 40 Ideas for sharing the Good News* (Board of National Mission, Church of Scotland).

- the giving of money;
- the giving of practical help;
- the giving of love.

Service starts on the congregation's own doorstep. The Session needs to be alert to the concerns and needs of its own locality. This can be done more easily in some areas than in others, where for example the geographical area or community to be served is clearly defined. However, some of the most imaginative ventures in service have occurred where the Church has had to discover the community for itself. For example:

- in town centre settings;
- amongst shops and offices;
- in widely-scattered rural areas;
- in meeting the special needs of the handicapped or the elderly.

Many examples of service in the neighbourhood are readily available and identifiable: special offerings for good causes, distribution of Harvest and Christmas gifts, organising outings for the elderly and housebound, providing volunteers for various charitable activities.

Sometimes local matters take on a sharper edge and it may be necessary to touch on concerns that are broadly 'political'. For instance, stating an opinion on or offering a protest about:

- the closure of a local industry;
- some new planning development;
- a particular local government policy;
- local education facilities, or the lack of them.

This can be controversial, but there are occasions when the Church has to stand up and be counted, and the leaders of the Church, especially at a local level, have a duty to do so. Service also involves concern for wider issues, on both the national and the international stage. Many Christians are increasingly interested in the big political and economic issues of our day – war and peace, law and order, poverty and wealth, energy and conservation.

Opportunities can arise for Sessions to comment upon such issues, or simply to discuss the principles involved in these important questions. Not all elders think that this should be done, but we believe that behind these topics lie moral principles and values that are of major importance. As Christians we should have something to say on such principles. If we don't, we run the risk of not being taken seriously at all.

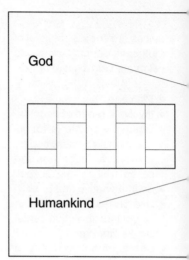

Wider links

Let us be concerned with one another, to help one another to show love and to do good. Let us not give up the habit of meeting together, as some are doing. Instead, let us encourage one another. Hebrews 10:24-25

To be true to the universal nature of its faith, the local church must maintain its links with its own denomination and the world Church. This is not only a confessional requirement, but a positive necessity for a healthy congregation. Without a deliberate effort to maintain such links a congregation can become isolated and introverted.

Certain duties are laid upon the Session in this respect by its superior courts. In the Church of Scotland, for example, a representative elder must be appointed annually to Presbytery. Usually this representative will report back at regular intervals to the Session. There may be specific reports and responses which the Presbytery requires of Sessions from time to time: for example, at the periodic visits to the congregation by representatives of the Presbytery.

An elder from each Session will also be nominated as a commissioner to the General Assembly in accordance with the local Presbytery rota. A Session is duty-bound to attend to the reports and deliverances

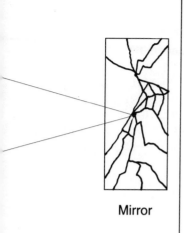

Mirror

In the Church of Scotland, the Church and Nation Committee, Board of World Mission and Unity and the Committee on Ecumenical Affairs can provide materials highlighting many of the issues and suggested responses to them.

of its Assembly and to carry out any actions required by it. The extent to which this requirement is heeded depends upon the strength of the wording in the Assembly deliverance.

In other Reformed traditions there are variations to these procedures. In all Presbyterian churches, however, the work of the Session must relate to its higher courts.

Other links may be less formal, but are of no less importance and value:

1 Links with associations of churches of the same denomination to provide joint services or acting as a general Session.
2 Links with local councils of churches and other ecumenical organisations which bring together denominations for general or specific purposes: for example, Holy Week services, Christian Aid fund-raising.
3 Links with the Church overseas through missionary partners, sponsoring relief agencies, developing visits and exchanges.

We are very conscious that the image which the Church presents to the world is often that of a shattered mirror which prevents mankind from seeing God clearly (▲ see diagram, top centre).

Whatever Sessions can do to restore the mirror to wholeness by developing these wider links will be vital to bringing humankind and God closer together.

Maintenance

Under [Christ's] control all the different parts of the body fit together and the whole body is held together by every joint with which it is provided. When each part works as it should the whole body grows ....

Ephesians 4:16

A Session needs to keep itself in good running order,

to maintain itself and its activities at peak performance. Maintenance in this positive sense is not to be confused with simply 'ticking over'. Rather, it is a necessary means by which leadership activity is sustained and expanded, by which the life of the Session and congregation is renewed.

Church law requires Sessions to maintain certain records and make certain statistical and other returns. Many of these involve routine administrative chores and gathering of information, often carried out by a particular office-bearer, usually the clerk or the roll-keeper. As a body, however, the Session should be aware of what is contained in these schedules and could develop ways of making use of this information.

The important business of maintaining the membership of the congregation is another continuing task of the Session. This is done in a number of ways:

1 Judging the suitability of new communicants and admitting new members to the congregation.
2 Ensuring that all members of the congregation are informed as to the duties and responsibilities of Church membership.
3 Maintaining a full and accurate roll of members, including a supplementary roll of those removed from the communion roll, but still residing in the district.

The traditional term for the Session's work in this sphere is 'discipline'. Today this implies less the stern imposition of punishment and more the sympathetic encouragement of the highest possible standards of membership. Sessions should be very aware of the need for this. (See *Session Matters* p 44).

Provision of material resources is another major aspect of maintenance. Making sure that the means are available to keep the local church running is a necessary part of leadership. These means include adequate financial resources, suitably maintained buildings, materials for congregational activities, proper structures and organisation.

UNDER [CHRIST'S] CONTROL ALL THE DIFFERENT PARTS OF THE BODY FIT TOGETHER AND THE WHOLE BODY IS HELD TOGETHER BY EVERY JOINT WITH WHICH IT IS PROVIDED. WHEN EACH PART WORKS AS IT SHOULD THE WHOLE BODY GROWS.

EPHESIANS 4:16

The relationship of the Session to such activities depends upon the constitutional system deployed. Three main forms exist:

1 The Session itself may deal with finance and property.
2 There may be a board for finance and property composed partly of elders and partly of elected members: for example, Congregational Board or Deacons Court.
3 Finance and property may be the remit of a separate congregationally-elected committee: for example, Committee of Management.

Nonetheless, the Session will retain some residual authority in these areas, irrespective of the precise format.

Finance and property can consume an inordinate amount of time and energy, to such an extent that they might swamp other matters. This is a sphere in which the distinction between 'capital B'-business and 'small b'-business has to be clearly perceived. Their importance has to be seen in perspective. These are means to goals rather than goals in themselves.

Keeping an eye on how well the Session's structure and organisation is working is also important. It is a task often left to the whims of the minister or clerk, or is not done at all. But it is useful to have some mechanism which regularly monitors the working arrangements, spots deficiencies and suggests improvements (see chapter 5). Thus the Session leadership can be kept up-to-date and forward-looking.

> The Church of Scotland Board of Stewardship and Finance have two programmes available: 'Christian Commitment' and 'Sharing Resources'.

Initiative and reaction

Any Session which takes these goals seriously will never have any lack of Business, for the promotion of Christ's Kingdom is a demanding process.

Yet many elders do complain of a lack of Session activity. Some Sessions meet very irregularly. Others squeeze in their meetings before or after other events.

Equally, there are frequent cries of protest about the amount of business created for Sessions by higher courts. A lot of time can be spent merely reacting to the requirements of other bodies.

This dilemma is part of the crisis of leadership which is commonly experienced by many elders. Too often Sessions appear to be pushed into half-hearted action by external events, the enthusiasms of the minister, or the complaints of individuals in the congregation. There is a clear distrust of centralised power and decision-making.

On the other hand, there is often no obvious willingness by Sessions to take the initiative themselves. Indeed there seems almost to be resistance to taking the lead. This appears to reflect a lack of awareness and confidence which prevents elders from being open to each other and to God's Spirit in the Church and in the world.

The numbers game

Part of the difficulty lies in the question of numbers. 'That's all very well for big Sessions', is the response, 'but we've only got eight elders. What can *we* do?'

Many Sessions are small – because of geographical factors, the nature of the community in which they operate, or because of the weakness of the congregation. This can often be a matter for depression and despair.

The responsiveness of a Session, however, is more a matter of attitude than of numbers. The Christian faith has always preached the importance of quality over quantity. Where there is a will to follow where God's Spirit is leading, a way will be found to shape circumstances to the size of the Session.

For example, a small Session can achieve a real informality and openness between its members which allows a deeper fellowship than is possible in a very large group.

Tasks which in a large Session might require a

HOW BIG DOES A LEADER-
SHIP TEAM NEED TO BE?
THE GOSPEL'S ANSWER CAN
BE SEEN IN THE EXAMPLE OF
JESUS – HE ONLY NEEDED
TWELVE DISCIPLES TO
ATTEMPT HIS TASK.

sizable group to work on can be taken up in small Sessions by individual elders or by working in pairs.

The local knowledge of a small Session might be considerable and the talents of other members of the congregation could be more readily utilised. For instance, Christian education in a small congregation need not be the concern only of elders. A working party of say two members of Session may work alongside a representative from the Woman's Guild, a Sunday School teacher, and a member of the congregation interested or gifted in this area. Large Sessions could also follow this line of participation.

How big does a leadership team need to be? The Gospel's answer can be seen in the example of Jesus – he only needed twelve disciples to attempt his task.

Congregational needs

It is also important to remember that the task of the Session is to lead the whole people of God in that place. The congregation is the focus of a Session's leadership, and it is to allow the congregation to exercise its ministry that the Session's work should be geared.

For this to happen the congregation must have some influence on the goals being pursued. The main example of this will be the annual congregational meeting, although in the United Reformed Church the activities of the elders are more regularly account-able to the Church meeting.

Whilst most Sessions are probably fairly represen-tative of the households and families within a congre-gation, this link should not be taken for granted. An openness to what the members of the Church family are thinking, and feeling, and needing is important to the development of a lively and meaningful Christian community.

So the Session should relate to its congregation to a degree where it is able to support and encourage initiatives wherever they come from, to formulate plans not just on the basis of what a few elders wish, but of what the whole congregation needs.

True ministry

We believe that the root of this issue lies in the failure to grasp the true nature of the shared ministry to which elders are called. Elders need to be encouraged to understand that their leadership involves taking responsibility and making decisions.

Sessions need to pursue their goals with positive initiative rather than tired reaction. Then congregations might start on the journey of becoming the exciting and attractive groups which God's people are meant to be.

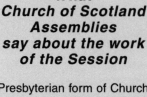

What Church of Scotland Assemblies say about the work of the Session

Presbyterian form of Church government involves a hierarchy of courts composed of ordained ministers and elders, rising from the Session at local congregational level to the national or General Assembly. At its annual meeting, the Assembly takes a number of decisions which commend certain actions to Sessions, or which require certain responses from them. These deliverances are one means by which the work of the Session is defined and reflects the views of successive Assemblies as to the appropriate leadership tasks of Sessions.

A study of Church of Scotland General Assembly deliverances indicates a range of matters sent to Sessions across the spectrum of leadership goals identified in our main text (see following pages).

ASSEMBLY AND SESSION

Christian education

A considerable stimulus to Session activity has come in this area in recent times, including concern for children and young people.

... for children and young people:
The Assembly

urge Kirk sessions to treat youth work as a priority claim and appeal to them to process the necessary resources to promote vigorously all aspects of youth work. (1992)

urge Kirk sessions to embark on study and discussion of the question of the admission of children to holy communion and draw attention to the fact that a series of study booklets is available. (1990)

... but adult education has also received due attention:
The Assembly

commend the new *Frontline* material for the training of first communicants to ministers and Kirk Sessions. (1992)

endorse the need for the engagement of adults in learning together about and developing in the Christian Faith and encourage all congregations to develop ways and means of promoting this objective. (1994)

... the training of church workers is another important part of education according to the Assembly:
The Assembly

urge all Kirk Sessions to encourage those in their congregations who teach the young to undergo periodic training especially through the Church's National Certificate programme. (1992)

encourages all elders to take advantage of the opportunities for further training provided at Presbytery and national level. (1983)

[To enable this latter work to be done the Church of Scotland set up the Eldership Working Party in 1980 to develop eldership training programmes. There are now over 40 elder trainers established in Presbyteries nation-wide.]

Christian Fellowship and Pastoral Care

Matters of worship and doctrine are mentioned surprisingly little in Assembly references to Kirk Sessions, but in 1990 –
The Assembly

instruct Kirk Sessions to study the draft Statement of Faith and the accompanying commentary, directing that comments be submitted through Presbyteries by 30th November 1991.

[There have been some attempts to direct the attention of sessions to particular groups within the congregation and to encourage a positive Christian lifestyle.]

The Assembly

welcome the publication of the new confirmation programme for use with

ASSEMBLY AND SESSION (cont'd)

persons with learning disabilities and commend the use of the programme to all congregations as appropriate. (1993)

invite the Board of National Mission to make available simple material providing advice to ministers, property conveners and elders to assist them in aiding communication with the deaf, deafened and hard of hearing. (1994)

Evangelism and Service

The Assembly

urge Kirk Sessions in the light of the statistical and social analysis to give urgent action and attention to the evangelisation of their parishes, and the developing of people, strategies and structures for the task of pastoral evangelism in line with 'Developing the Missionary Parish'. (1989)

urge Kirk Sessions to study the section 'The Evangelistic Challenge of Scotland Today' and to respond to it wherever possible in co-operation with local denominations. (1989)

encourage Kirk Sessions to set and work for goals including arrangements for nurture of new Christians and with particular emphasis on the need to have a well-founded Biblical faith especially seeking new members by profession of faith. (1994)

encourage Kirk sessions to explore the opportunities and developments which Community radio provides for strengthening community spirit and outreach in their areas. (1990)

urge Kirk Sessions to take specific initiatives, whether through political representations or corporate or individual action, to address the needs of the poor in their area. (1990)

invite Kirk sessions to consider the environmental impact of businesses in their community and to encourage good practice. (1994)

encourage Kirk sessions to ensure that the guidelines in 'Racism and the Church – A Guide To Good Practice' are implemented throughout the whole Church. (1994)

commend the report on Crime and Punishment for discussion by Kirk Sessions and Congregations. (1994)

urge Kirk Sessions to encourage parents, teachers and further education lecturers with all church members to take an interest in their School and College Boards, to be ready to offer themselves for service on them and to do all they can to ensure adequate staffing and resourcing of Religious Education: and note with concern the difficulties which will be created and will continue in Scotland's rural schools by the introduction of school boards. (1989)

urge church members in leadership positions in small and medium sized businesses to volunteer their services for local agencies of Scottish Enterprise in order that real benefits may be derived from it. (1989)

ASSEMBLY AND SESSION (cont'd)

Wider Links

The Assembly

encourage congregations to develop their parish magazines as an effective tool for communication. (1993)

commend *Life and Work* to congregations as a means of learning about the Church and its work. (1994)

urge all congregations to make use of the audio-visual material produced by Pathway Productions. (1993)

urge Kirk sessions to draw the attention of congregations to the challenging opportunities for overseas service with partner churches, who are engaged in costly witness for the Good News of Christ, often in situations of great economic hardship, in Africa, Asia, the Middle East and the Caribbean. (1990)

urge Kirk Sessions to pray for suitably qualified men and women who will offer to serve with our partner churches and especially for the doctors needed in Malawi and Kenya. (1992)

encourage congregations to enter into twinning arrangements with congregations in Eastern and Western Europe. (1989)

Local Mission, Local Ministry and the Mission and Aid Fund. (1993)

commend the work of Stewardship Promoters and urge office bearers to support and encourage Promoters as they seek to fulfil their role in the life of the congregation. (1992)

commend the Christian Commitment and Sharing Resources Programmes and urge congregations to undertake regular stewardship reviews. (1994)

commend to congregations the manual on heating and lighting church buildings known as *Heat and Light* and remind congregations that for a modest fee, towards which the General Trustees offer a subsidy, expert advice can be obtained on how to save money on fuel costs and/or improve the standard of comfort in buildings. (1994)

encourage Kirk Sessions to discuss the issues raised in the popular pamphlet, arising out of the Interim Report on 'Decline of Numbers of Young People in the Church' and invite response. (1994)

Maintenance

The Assembly

urge Kirk Sessions and Financial Boards to place before their members the need for and the privilege of regular, sacrificial giving to support the work of

[The above quotations are taken from the Reports to the General Assembly or *Blue Books*. The year is given in brackets.]

Conflicting loyalties

In Cox's *Practice and Procedure in The Church of Scotland* we read: *'As "pastors and doctors" should be diligent in sowing the seed of the Word, so the elders should be careful in seeking the fruit of it in the people.'* Also: *'The office of elder is severally and conjunctly to watch over the flock committed to their charge, both publicly and privately, that no corruption of religion or manners enter therein.'*

Apart from the old-fashioned language that sounds good, though we may feel a bit uneasy about the 'corruption' bit. Our unease may be increased by the following from Cox: *'Elders ought to bring to the Kirk Session things they cannot correct by private admonition.'*

We tend to shy away from this in a way that generations ago did not. In a more puritanical age we dealt as elders with 'scandals' like swearing, cursing, profaning the Lord's Day, drunkenness, sexual sins. Discipline was high on our agenda. Should it be so today? Perhaps it should, but in no way would I wish to return to the days when, *eg*, unmarried mothers took their infants for baptism to what was considered the more kindly Episcopal Church ('the Kirk where they baptise a' the bairns') or when ministers were reprimanded for 'promiscuous invitations' to Communion!

Few of us would wish to return to the days which gave the Kirk such a stern and negative image, but what do we do with congregation members who demonstrate remarkably little interest in its life and witness, including its Sunday worship? If we have done our best to surface the real issues and have offered whatever help we can to no avail, what then?

Cox tells us: *'The Kirk Session shall have power, at the annual revision of the Communion Roll, to remove from the Roll the names of persons who are giving no evidence of real interest or are taking no share in the Church's Work and Worship.'*

Many Sessions and elders feel very hesitant about this exercise of discipline and so our Communion Rolls often contain the names of many who are showing 'no real interest .... '

It seems to me that we have a problem of conflicting loyalties. There are members who are over-burdened or disheartened because of lack of support from the 'no clear interests', and members who might become more involved but for the witness of the disinterested.

Our acceptance of the standards of the 'no clear interests' does not help them to take the Faith and Church seriously.

Perhaps most serious of all is the obstacle the 'no clear interests' may present to the encouragement of those outside the Church. It is not easy to persuade someone to become interested in Christ and his Church when he watches a neighbour, who is a 'member', cutting the lawn on Sunday mornings except on the odd Communion Sunday.

An indisciplined congregation may not be an attractive one.

3

COMMON PROBLEMS

Does your Session suffer from any of the following:

* misunderstandings?
* power struggles?
* hidden agendas?
    deeper, unspoken issues being hidden in your
    discussions?

* meetings after the meetings?
* lack of confidentiality?
* poor decision-making?
    agreeing things, but without a personal com-
    mitment to the implications?

* boredom?
* infrequent meetings?
    the same two or three people doing all the talking?

If the answer is 'yes ' to a fair number of these then,
    despite the fact that ...

* life is about relationships,
* the Gospel about at-one-ment,
* and the Church about fellowship ...

then you as a Session are experiencing the kind of
problems that are frequently present among those
who have not done enough baseline thinking.

Discussions with ministers, session clerks and
numerous other elders have helped us to identify a
number of key areas in which problems commonly
occur.

1 *Lack of clear purpose*

A clear vision of the job is often lacking. Elders are not always sure of what their job is in practical terms. This can show itself in a tendency to emphasise 'status' rather than responsibility. It can be seen in a rigid sticking to the 'letter of the law' as laid down in regulations and acts, rather than in creativity and initiative.

2 *Lack of motivation*

Elders may not show any desire to do the job properly. This can be seen in instances of absenteeism, apathy, inequalities in sharing workloads, and 'letterbox' pastoral work.

3 *Personal differences*

People have different personalities, views and styles of behaviour which can produce problems. Personality differences, cliques and warring factions can produce open conflict which may tear a Session apart or simmer below the surface, hampering openness to God, to each other, and to the tasks of leadership.

4 *Size*

Size can be a problem – either because there are thought to be too few elders or because the Session is very large. Small Sessions may feel under great pressure through shortage of personnel, or may automatically reject certain possibilities as only open to those with more elders. The result may be apathy or inaction. Equally, in a large group it is unlikely that many will feel free to speak out, though they may have plenty to say outside the Session Room. It is easier in a large Session to 'hide', thus avoiding a fair share of work and responsibility.

5 *Poor conduct of meetings*

The way in which the Session meeting operates may blunt and kill participation so that elders don't attend, or say nothing when they do. Ministers, clerks and other dominant figures may deny involvement to others and go unchallenged by the silent majority. The purpose of a meeting may be unclear and ill-prepared, allowing 'red herrings' to be chased and 'garden paths' to be followed. This can be seen particularly on occasions when feet are rumbled in acceptance of a proposal, but the implementation is somebody else's responsibility.

6 *Negative attitudes*

Is your Moderator really the moderator of the creativity and enthusiasm of your elders?

It may be that the enthusiasms of your minister and other members of your Session are being curbed by various 'moderators' whose attitudes are geared to ensuring that no change is permitted, no activity or adventure allowed, and the attitude of 'we never did it that way before' rules.

The problem of change

Change is a major cause of many of the problems which we face as individuals and in our Sessions to-day. Change comes at us from a wide range of sources and at a tremendous rate.

Economic changes affect the financial viability of many congregations: heating costs rise; stipends lose value; levels of giving fail to keep pace with our needs.

Employment changes affect people's lifestyle in relation to the Church's traditional patterns of worship and witness: weekend working; redundancy and loss of employment; greater mobility as people follow jobs; increasing holidays and leisure time.

Social patterns of how people live affect the impact

'What possible reason is there for saying I don't seem very receptive to new ideas?'

of the Church on people's lives: the loss of community spirit in many places; the housing patterns of high-rise flats and large estates; rural depopulation, especially as young people move away for or after school; changing roles for men and women.

Technological changes produce new ways of doing things almost overnight: the impact of television and video; the decline in literary forms of communication; the greater technical sophistication of young people.

Educational changes affect people's attitudes: modern teaching techniques encourage a questioning approach, participation and involvement; belief can be challenged; mere acceptance of authority is lessened.

Ethical changes also occur to challenge orthodox morality and ways of thinking: increasing breakdowns in marriage and family life; 'permissive' sexual behaviour; more one-parent families; more overtly atheistic beliefs.

Resistance

Change produces a common predictable reaction – resistance. This can be very true in the Church. Many members can find it hard to adapt to change.

Many Christians can see themselves as an increasingly beleaguered minority in society and can tend to become more and more defensive.

Resistance to change is natural and is based upon a number of factors:

1 Change is often seen as being impersonal, from the outside and beyond the control of the individual.

2 Change usually disrupts existing patterns of relationships and structures; change alters well-established ways of doing things; change causes personal inconvenience.

CHANGE IS A MAJOR CAUSE OF MANY OF THE PROBLEMS WHICH WE FACE AS INDIVIDUALS AND IN OUR SESSIONS TODAY.

3 Change undermines self-confidence because existing skills or knowledge and past experience built up over a long period of time are counted worthless; change means the need to start again; change means learning new skills and relationships.

4 Change creates fear, uncertainty and insecurity; change means the removal of things that are familiar and their replacement with things that are unfamiliar; change means a leap into the unknown.

Challenge and opportunity

It is a pity that change is so often seen only as a threat. In many instances it can be viewed as a challenge and can present many positive opportunities to the leadership of the local congregation.

Economic changes might encourage the Session to look more carefully at what its goals are and how to utilise its resources to the fullest potential. This could lead to raising the standards of membership.

Social changes might present the Session with the opportunity to think about how best the needs of people might be catered for. This could lead to new patterns of worship and fellowship and evangelism.

Technological changes provide new aids to make congregational administration easier or more effective. Computers can be used regarding finance, pastoral care, education – as can the medium of video.

Educational changes can provide us with new opportunities in colleges, schools and congregations to confront life's religious questions and seek the insights of the Gospel.

To erect barricades against all change does not seem to us to be either a very helpful or very Christian attitude.

Lack of confidence

It is obvious to us that many elders are seriously lacking in confidence and feel personally inadequate.
This may in fact be the basic problem facing elders
and Sessions. This is not surprising in these rapidly
changing times. But we believe that this lack of confidence and the various problems outlined above also
stem from:

- a lack of *Baseline thinking;*
- an inadequate understanding of the Session's
  Leadership role
- insufficient emphasis on building Session
  Teamwork;
- inefficient Team management.

To these latter two matters we now turn.

SESSION MATTERS

SESSION MATTERS

Feeling inadequate?

Some time ago I was greatly saddened – not for him, but for those of us who loved him – by the sudden, unexpected death of an elder who had been a friend and fellow-worker. We had spent many a youth weekend together, shared many a pastoral concern and worked well together in the leadership of our congregation.

Though highly respected by his fellow elders, the folks in his district and young people he served as a youth leader, Alex often felt inadequate about being an elder. He was anything but.

An elder with a district to care for has a great calling. Real pastoral concern takes time, sensitivity, devotion, freely given year in and year out. Such devotion is not always appreciated. It can be taken for granted. Sometimes it has to face put-downs and discouragements: homes that refuse entry; complaints and excuses made over and over again; promises made but never kept. Such responses invite us to blame ourselves, feel a failure, feel inadequate.

In my experience many a fine elder and effective Christian feels inadequate. And what is true of an individual elder can also be true of a Session. When as a Session we are trying to give real, creative leadership to our congregation and meeting with little response; when we are trying to provide opportunities for worship, support, learning, service and meeting with great indifference, we can feel very inadequate.

Regarding our feelings it is useful to remember that we choose how we feel. People can invite us to feel good or bad, but it is we who decide what we are going to feel. We have the power to decide how we are to respond to discouragement.

It is also useful to keep in mind that it is our responsibility (individually and collectively) to offer the best we can; it is other people's responsibility what they do with it. This I find a great safeguard against apathy. We have to offer the best we can. It is also a safeguard against carrying the burden of other people's responsibility. If we are sincerely doing what we can for God and his people, that is all God expects of us. How others respond is between them and God. That is not our burden.

Doing our best is, of course, not easy. It is costly. Eldership is no light-weight responsibility. When I feel inadequate I find comfort and strength in the recognition that so many of the leaders of God's people in the Bible were clearly flawed people, people inadequate in many ways, but people through whom God could achieve much. What he did with them he can do with us.

4

TEAMWORK

In training programmes conducted for elders all over Scotland we have found that elders, in every kind of setting (from inner city to outer isles) have warmed to the understanding of the Session as the leadership *team* of the congregation.

We ask them to work out in small groups of six or seven what the essentials are for any team (for example, a football team or a hockey team) to permit it to play as well as it can and have a chance of winning. Again and again, in as little as six minutes, collectively these groups have come up with almost all the items in the 'Essentials of Teamwork' box on p 54.

The problem of transference

Every group to date, without exception, has said that training is an essential for a team to play as well as it can and have a chance of winning. When we then ask them to outline the training programme they have established in their own Session, there is usually a pregnant silence. The silence intensifies if we ask:

- How do you go about developing your Session's understanding of the 'game' it is called to play?
  or
- What do you do to develop mutual support and understanding in your Session?

We do not need to teach our fellow elders about teamwork. They know the answers. The problem, however, is the problem of transference. Although the idea of the Session as the leadership team is readily grasped and warmly responded to, what is known about teamwork in the context of sport is not being transferred, applied, to our work as Sessions.

Often the way we do things destroys, or at least impedes, the development of teamwork. If we believe that Christian fellowship should be a marked characteristic of a congregation and we want to develop a congregation's shared ministry, then fellowship and teamwork within the Session have to be priorities

This is further underlined when we consider the purpose of the Church, its mission, and the necessary leadership goals of a Session. Serious consideration has therefore to be given to the following matters.

Basic fitness

While it is true that throughout history elders have been usually senior in years, it is not true that this needs to be the case.

The fact is that people mature at very different rates, and whereas some people of fifty are still rather childish, some people of twenty are fully mature. It is better to judge people individually, rather than to have an inflexible age limit. Stephen Mayor

It matters is that we appoint elders, of whatever age or gender, who are mature and maturing Christians.

Attention was drawn on page 7 to Numbers 11 where it states that elders are to be appointed for the People of God on the basis of recognised and respected leadership qualities. The lifestyle of the congregation is very important. There has to be good soil in which future leaders can be cultivated and be equipped with a living Christian faith and basic leadership skills.

ELDERS DON'T NEED TO BE SENIOR IN YEARS – WHAT MATTERS IS THAT THEY ARE MATURE AND MATURING CHRISTIANS.

Good selection and preparation procedures

The whole idea of effective teamwork can be lost at this

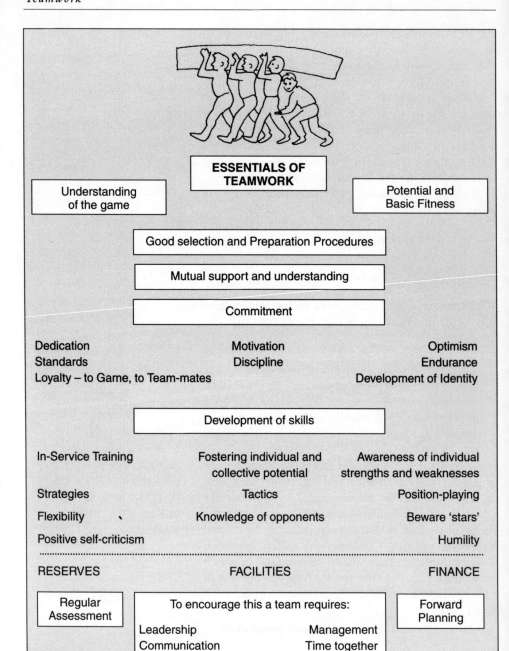

ESSENTIALS OF TEAMWORK

Understanding of the game

Potential and Basic Fitness

Good selection and Preparation Procedures

Mutual support and understanding

Commitment

Dedication	Motivation	Optimism
Standards	Discipline	Endurance
Loyalty – to Game, to Team-mates		Development of Identity

Development of skills

In-Service Training	Fostering individual and collective potential	Awareness of individual strengths and weaknesses
Strategies	Tactics	Position-playing
Flexibility	Knowledge of opponents	Beware 'stars'
Positive self-criticism		Humility

RESERVES   FACILITIES   FINANCE

Regular Assessment

To encourage this a team requires:

Leadership   Management
Communication   Time together

Forward Planning

point. How many elders do we need? Typical answer:

Roll of members	1500
Members' homes	990
Agreed number per elder	15
Therefore elders required	66
Present strength	55
Therefore appoint	11

Therefore, choose 15 and hope 11 will accept!

Governing factor: pastoral coverage; whether meaningfully understood or not. *Ignores:* homes of lapsed members; homes of non-members; use of non-Session visitors; other leadership roles.

Such a procedure is made worse when the choice of new elders is made by a Session that does not know the person in depth and when standards are employed which would be totally unacceptable, if we change the analogy to the world of business, to a firm selling confectionery!

The failure is further compounded by the elected person receiving only a 'chat with the minister' prior to coming to his/her decision and possible ordination. In our experience this is sadly common.

Surely for such an important leadership task, the leading of the ministry of the congregation, there requires to be a serious preparation programme – not just for the job, but for the making of a meaningful response ('Yes' or 'No') to the invitation and challenge to join the leadership team.

Vows akin to marriage are to be taken. It is irresponsible to invite people to take them without doing our level best to help them to understand what it is they are being asked to do.

The model on page 57-58 is one Session's attempt to devise a meaningful selection procedure. It helped to overcome various 'bad' practices and gives various useful pointers to other Sessions. This Session, however, numbered 25. The procedure might prove more difficult to operate in a larger Session.

If the congregation is to be involved in the procedure, the following could be adopted:

1 The Session decides to add to its number. A list of things to look for in candidates is drawn up:

   • personal faith in and love for God;
   • involvement in the worship and work of the congregation;
   • particular gifts and experience, leadership potential, ability to work with others;
   • availability to serve.

2 Sheets indicating these criteria are issued to the congregation and names are requested. At this stage, it should be made clear that such names are only recommendations.

3 The Session receives the list of names from members, without any indication of the number of nominations each has received. Elders can then add their own recommendations. The list is remitted to a small working group.

4 Having consulted and deliberated, the group reports back to the Session with a list of those to be approached. The Session decides to accept, reject, add or subtract.

5 Approaches are made to the persons on the list by the moderator and the respective district elder. The approach is, 'Are you willing to undertake a period of preparation with a view to becoming an elder?'

6 A number of preparation sessions are held. These would normally include such topics as:

   • What is a Christian?
   • What is the Church for?
   • What does an elder do?
   • How does the Session work?
   • How do you look after a district?
   • What is involved in ordination?

MODEL FOR ACTION

Selection procedure

The Session had always used the method of electing elders by nomination and decision of the Session itself. Any system is open to error but we saw no reason to change this procedure. Together, however, we evolved the following decision process.

At the Session meeting following the one at which it had been decided to add to our numbers, names were suggested for prayerful consideration, but on the clear understanding that no discussion would take place at this stage with any of the people concerned. There is no need to embarrass someone by a rejection. It was agreed that the election would take place at the next meeting of Session.

On the evening of the election Session reminded itself of three things:

1 The confidential nature of what was to take place and that any breach of confidence would require to be explained to the Session. It is vitally important that each elder feels free to speak as he/she feels.

2 The importance of what we were about to do, not least for those we might ask to consider taking the vows of eldership which are akin to marriage vows .

3 There being in our judgement no precise number that required to be reached, the people who would be nominated were in no way in competition with each other.

Nominations were then called for with a brief comment to justify the nomination. A list was formed of those who received a seconder.

Attention was then turned on the first person on the list.

The nominator and seconder were invited to speak. Full and frank discussion followed. When Session felt ready to undertake the first vote each elder was able to vote:

- For the nomination;
- Against the nomination;
- Don't know that the time is right;
- Don't know the person.

The 'Don't know the time is right' category permits support, but real pastoral concern for the person's present family circumstances, work situation or whatever else might place too heavy a burden on the person at this particular time.

The 'Don't know the person' allows escape from a 'For' vote simply because it appears unkind to oppose a nomination.

The vote of the Session was charted for all to see. Then came the second vote. Each elder voted 'Elect' or 'Not elect' on the basis of judgement of the strength of Session opinion.

MODEL FOR ACTION (cont'd)

Before the voting had begun we had decided that if, for example, there were 22 of us present, 19 'Elect' votes would be required for a person to be approached. And so we moved slowly down the list.

These evenings were not short, but for all of us they were moving and fascinating experiences and had a bearing on the subsequent integration of new elders into the team.

This procedure rarely led to many approaches being made to people at any one time, but it meant that people were approached when the whole Session really believed them to have the potential to become committed and effective elders.

Procedure in outline

Session meeting: decision to elect.

Session meeting: possible candidates listed for consideration.
NB: no approaches to be made.

Session meeting: **election**
three reminders: importance, confidentiality, no fixed number and decision *re* second vote.
Nominators – seconders → list (brief word).
(fuller word – supporting statement – discussion)

First vote: Yes; No; Not at this time; Don't know the person.

Second vote: Elect; Not elect.

Final decision

Individual interviews (with minister) (1): Unspecified time for consideration.

Individual interviews (2): Further time if required.

Individual interviews (3): decision as to whether or not to embark on open-ended preparation course.

Preparation course (five meetings).

Individual interviews (4): Further time if required.

Final interview (if required).

Session meeting: Report.
Decisions *re*: Ordination date.
Time span: at least six months.

Elder contract

An elder in this congregation is expected to do his/her best to meet the following commitments:

1 To be at worship on Sunday mornings unless working, ill or out of town.
2 To be regular in attendance at Session meetings and to send an apology if absent.
3 To share in the work of Session committees.
4 To recognise and support the Session's positive role in promoting the Christian good of the congregation and parish.
5 To carry out Welcome Duty as per rota.
6 To attend the service at our mission station at least once per year.
7 To share in the Communion duties.
8 To have a deed of covenant, if a tax-payer.
9 To care for his/her district: (a) by regular visits into each home; (b) by praying regularly for the members of the district by name; (c) by sharing any difficulties with the minister; (d) by sharing with the minister in cases of extra need, *eg* bereavement, illness or a baptism.

7 At this point the prospective elders decide whether they wish to proceed to ordination and the Session makes the necessary arrangements for their ordination and admission.

In this way, what is expected of those who take on the job of elder is clearly defined, adequate training is given, and enough time is allowed for considered decisions to be made.

Contract

We believe that it is important for a Session to establish a contract which clearly and unambiguously sets out what the Session expects a new member to do in the fulfilment of the vow of ordination in the congregation it leads.

Problems can clearly arise when a Session begins to ask more of members who have been brought in on a light-weight or largely unspoken contract.

The provision of good in-service training and mutual support structures are important in this regard, as indeed they are for the whole development of teamwork.

Training

In chapter 2 we tried to outline the leadership task of the Session. For this task training is essential. Even if we think only of the pastoral task – the responsibility for going into homes to care for people in all sorts of joys and difficulties – training is a must.

Real pastoral concern – the sharing of the joys and difficulties of our fellow-Christians in the intimacy of their own homes, where often there are non-Christians – calls for relationship skills.

We need training:

- in understanding behaviour, other people's and our own;

SESSION MATTERS

SESSION MATTERS

When the team works together

I heard that on the date of our next Session meeting Scotland would be playing a match in the World Cup. I knew that most of the elders, like most of Scotland, would want to watch the match on television.

We had worked hard all winter on our team eldership (with the monthly house church as its focal point), on our annual stewardship programme and on the other things an active Session gets involved in. I decided to ask the Session if it wished to alter the date of our next meeting.

'Moderator,' a voice asked, 'when does the Session meet?'

'The last Wednesday of each month,' I replied.

'Then, Moderator, that's when the Session will meet.' And so said they all.

On the evening in question, when many in Scotland were glued to their television sets, over ninety per cent of our Session assembled for our monthly meeting. Apologies had been received from those who

were on the back-shift. Only one elder was missing and unaccounted for.

As I looked round at the Session I remembered advice I'd been given some years earlier – I should not expect a high turn-out if the local football team was playing at home on the Session night.

I remembered also the days when, for some, 9 o' clock seemed to have some 'tablets of stone' significance regardless of the importance of the work in hand; and I realised that we had learned together over the years that 22 men kicking a ball was not comparable to the meaningfulness, challenge and fun of the Session meeting.

A minister, on learning that somewhere it was written that in heaven there were to be four and twenty elders, decided that he didn't want to go. As a parish minister I have shared that feeling! However I can honestly say that the aspect of the parish ministry I miss most, while at present not at work as a parish minister, is not being the moderator of a real Session team.

'There's nothing like knocking on a door to learn about visiting!'

WE NEED TRAINING:
IN UNDERSTANDING
BEHAVIOUR – OTHER
PEOPLE'S AND OUR OWN;
IN LEARNING TO LISTEN SO
THAT WE CAN HEAR AND
SEE WHAT IS NOT BEING
OPENLY SAID; IN SHARING
OUR FAITH EFFECTIVELY.

Training programme

Training began at Session meetings with Bible study, not just individual passages, but also looking at the Bible as a whole.

With the help of various resource people at day conferences, the purpose of the Church and the role of the Session were explored.

A major step forward was achieved when some elders took part in a residential weekend away from home on the theme of what Jesus means to each of us .

This residential event became annual. As the hunger for training grew, three 'split weekends' were added – Friday evening, plus Sunday afternoon ending with a meal together and evening service. Emphasis was placed on building relationships in the Session and on learning pastoral skills.

- in learning to listen so that we can hear and see what is not being openly said;
- in sharing our faith effectively.

Training can help us to understand, for example, the phases a bereaved person goes through, and so can help us to care meaningfully and to share our faith in appropriate ways. Experience can also be a good teacher.

There is nothing like knocking on a door to learn about visiting. But you learn even more if you discuss it afterwards with a person of experience, different experience, or greater experience.   I Strachan

We believe that training should be available to elders in three different settings:

1 in the local Session itself, within its ordinary meetings, at day conferences and week-end retreats;
2 at the presbytery level where elders from various congregations can get together to learn and share their experiences;
3 at the national level in residential situations where more in-depth learning opportunities can be provided and spiritual batteries be recharged over the extended period of at least a weekend.

Each of the above has something different to offer. Each Session should work out its own continuing programme. Every presbytery should provide at least an annual opportunity for the wider coming together of elders. Over and above these opportunities elders would benefit greatly from taking part, from time to time, in a nationally-led residential programme.

A team will have little chance of playing as well as it can, let alone winning, without a commitment to training. We would do well to write this commitment into our contract. *As we learn together, we build teamwork and confidence.*

Mutual support and understanding

It used to be said that a family that prayed together stayed together. A Session likewise must develop a spiritual depth, learning to pray together, open the Bible together, worship together, journey like Abraham together, and care deeply for one another.

It is important to develop very specific support structures for the elders, including the minister. All of us go through difficult times: family difficulties; personal illness; spiritually 'dry' periods; problems of conflicting commitments; times when we are unable to pull our weight fully; times when we need the support and understanding of the rest of the team.

The development of support structures is a sign of love for one another. It is important that we get the chance to talk to each other, to share our beliefs and opinions in an atmosphere of acceptance.

It is also important, perhaps even more important, that we get the opportunity to share our feelings. We find the diagram opposite helpful.

Much of our human communication does not get past levels 5 (generalities about the weather, football scores, *etc*) and 4 (talk in kindly or unkindly fashion about other people).

Level 3 is not uncommon. Indeed quite a number of us feel very free to give the world our opinions, be they well thought out or mere prejudices. Fellowship building requires getting beyond these levels.

The following quotation was written about Christian house groups, but it applies equally to a Session that is seeking to develop teamwork in Christ. Such a Session will find ways to:

> *enable members to get in touch with themselves, their feelings, their hopes and fears, and to share them in appropriate ways, if and when they wish to do so.*
> *This paves the way for peak communication or sharing. When someone shares something of themselves in depth, and is listened to and accepted in love, that person*

AS WE LEARN TOGETHER, WE BUILD TEAMWORK AND CONFIDENCE.

1   Peak
2   My feelings
3   My opinions, beliefs
4   Talk about other people
    Cliché (weather, *etc*)
5

JOHN POWELL, IN HIS BOOK *WHY AM I AFRAID TO TELL YOU WHO I AM?* OUTLINED THESE '5 LEVELS OF COMMUNICATION' (above).

A Model for Action

How can we best care for our elders, enabling them to carry out their duties effectively? That was the question asked by one Kirk Session, knowing that elders are supposed to look after their districts, but may find it hard. Some may have difficulty getting over the doorstep; others lose sleep worrying about district visiting.

The Session set up an 'Elder Support Group' consisting of the minister, Session clerk and 3 other elders (one recently ordained). It would be responsible for support rather than discipline and would not report back to the Session on individual cases.

The group did a basic eldership course at St Ninian's, a Church of Scotland residential training/resource centre. They had a series of training meetings with the Adviser in Elder Training looking at situations they might encounter and how to handle these.

The group now make periodic visits in pairs to elders. They listen to problems and give encouragement and practical help as required. They also meet together to discuss issues that have arisen and where appropriate take action.

experiences the Gospel and the Christ who is present when two or three are gathered together in his name.

In this process of sharing we discover ourselves, each other and the God who shares Himself with us. We discover trust and it is through faith that we experience salvation and new life. We learn to love, for that is the essence of the Gospel – the loving acceptance of ourselves, our neighbour and God. People in house groups often report a discovery, or rediscovery, of hope.

Growth is experienced out of the ground of faith, hope and love. The house group enables individuals to discover hidden potential and creativity within themselves – aspects of the image of God in which we were created ....

There is a great deal of learning from each other. There is the discovery of a new unity which goes beyond intellectual or theological agreement and is often experienced in spite of disagreement.

Ken Lawson
'The House Group Opportunity', *Frontline* A9

A Session which does not experience fellowship itself will not be able to promote it in the congregation. It will certainly be unlikely to try to foster it. It will also have difficulty with essentials like position-playing and flexibility.

In any team, *position-playing* is important. Players have different skills and these skills are required in different areas. Eleven centre-forwards may find they let in a lot of goals if they do not have a goal-keeper.

Flexibility can also be very important: 'I've been a right-back for ten years and I'm not going to change my position, even if we have ten right-backs and no wingers.'

That kind of common inflexibility is not conducive to good teamwork. As teamwork and confidence are fostered, such fearful selfishness diminishes.

It can also be useful to have the opportunity to relax together and to have *fun* together.

A Session which seeks to understand its purpose,

and to provide good selection and preparation procedures, sound mutual support structures, and in-service training will be able to meet the other 'Essentials' outlined on page 54 under the headings of Commitment and Development of Skills.

Forward planning and assessment

Sessions which are really largely involved in the status quo, 'ticking over' type of maintenance work, rarely get involved in *forward planning*. They miss the key question we should always keep before us: 'Where does God want us now to go as a people?' They should certainly keep before them the matter of regular *assessment*. We deal with this further in chapter 5 on Team Management.

In our experience elders tend to omit these essentials for a team to play as well as it can and have a chance of winning. If we were trying to win the World Cup we would be assessing our performance and planning our future strategies. Why then are Sessions, who 'play' for the Kingdom of God – so infinitely more important – often so slack and inefficient in their teamwork?

Time together

The building of teamwork takes time. A Session that meets four times a year can only, at best, achieve 'ticking over' maintenance.

To achieve the goals of a modern Session involves a real commitment of time and energy. No team can hope to win the World Cup, or any cup, with half the players in the dressing room! We have to encourage each other to take to the field with a will to win.

Leadership

We like the 'beware stars' comment on the 'Essentials' diagram (page 54). Particular skills can be extremely

SESSION LEADERSHIP IS A SHARED RESPONSIBILITY.

SESSION MATTERS

SESSION MATTERS

'Once an elder ... '

Some say, 'once an elder, always an elder.' Others say an elder's term of office should be limited, as the appointment of a manager to the congregational board is limited: with a fixed term of office.

In the Church of Scotland an elder is ordained, which signifies that we consider the appointment to the eldership to be on a different plane from, say, the appointment of a manager to the congregational board.

Accepting ordination is a serious step, entering upon a very important office within the Church. A person is ordained into a particular Session to exercise, with fellow-elders, spiritual leadership within a particular congregation. It should not be taken lightly or selfishly, but with reverence and dedication. The vows taken are, in my view, akin to the vows of marriage: just as long-term in their intention. We do not enter marriage on a three-year term of appointment basis, renewable or otherwise!

An elder can be removed from office. He or she can resign from Session and retain status as an elder as long as the resignation is simply accepted. An elder can also demit his status by making his request to his Session and by having the petition granted. This is possible, but it is surely not the intention for one who accepts the vows of ordination to the eldership.

Mamie was a senior citizen by the time of her ordination to the eldership. She was fit, active, a gem of a Christian. She belonged to a team eldership. The Session as a body was a team, but it also operated in area teams. Each elder had a district but worked with two or three other elders in a shared concern for their combined districts. Mamie belonged to her area team.

As time went by she became less able to visit her district. Evening calls, calls up flights of stairs were impossible. Others in the team took over. Eventually she had no pastoral calls to make, but she never left the team. The team would arrange for their monthly house group to be held in Mamie's house or they would transport her, and indeed others, who wanted to take part, to wherever the group was meeting in the area. Likewise she was brought to Session meetings where she contributed to our life by her presence and her warm support.

A few years ago Mamie died. Her funeral service was conducted in the sanctuary of her church. Her coffin was surrounded by her fellow-elders, brothers and sisters, sons and daughters in the faith – a rich family occasion. She had never resigned, not even retired. She died as an active elder. We would not have wanted it otherwise for her – or for ourselves.

valuable, but a 'star' is not a team, nor a team a 'star'.

A Session and congregation are often only good at what the minister is good at, and it can be 'all change' when a new minister arrives. A matter like the preparation of new elders should not be left to the minister alone. This is a shared responsibility.

Session leadership is a shared responsibility. Our leader is, of course, Jesus. He charts our course and helps us on our journey, if we are open to his leadership. In the Gospels we see Jesus setting people free and enabling them to achieve what they did not think possible for them.

A Session must be led with this understanding of *enabling*. In this regard the roles of the minister and Session clerk are very important. If this is given, then with all the collective talent and experience in a Session attuned to God's Spirit, creativity should abound. Such a Session will come to see its role in enabling the ministry of its whole congregation, imparting to the congregation the will to win.

If we take the understanding of shared ministry seriously, then the congregation as a whole is the 'team' and the Session is the leadership '*team of the team*'.

IF WE TAKE THE UNDER-STANDING OF SHARED MINISTRY SERIOUSLY, THEN THE CONGREGATION AS A WHOLE IS THE 'TEAM' AND THE SESSION IS THE LEADERSHIP 'TEAM OF THE TEAM'.

We believe that the development of a genuine teamwork in Christ would liberate the vast potential for leadership that exists in Sessions.

Many congregations may be lacking in missionary zeal because they are lacking in fellowship in Christ. Many Sessions may be lacking in the exercise of Christian leadership because they have not been working at becoming the Christian team our faith and form of government call for.

What we have been trying to say can now be summarised:

Life	**Relationships**	
	↓	
Christian faith	**At-one-ment**	
	↓	
Church	**Fellowship** ➡	**Mission**
	(Shared ministry)	
	↓	↓
Session	**Teamwork** ➡	**Leadership**

5

TEAM MANAGEMENT

Leading God's people is not only about the nature of leadership. It is about carrying out effective leadership. We do not want to build just any old team, but one which will have a chance of winning.

Management experts tend to agree that effective ways of achieving goals involve taking account of:

- *the task:* how the job is to be done;
- *the team:* how people feel;
- *the situation:* how external forces have influence.

Various names have been given to the best way to combine these factors successfully: *eg* 'democratic leadership style' (working alongside the group); or 'participatory management' (involving many people in decision-making). In some areas it is called 'corporate management' (a team approach); in others 'quality circles' (workers talking together about job improvements).

All of these stress the use of the abilities and commitment of everyone in the group in getting a job done. This helps to produce both general efficiency and individual satisfaction.

The term that we like to use, in line with our emphasis on the Session as the leadership team of the congregation, is *team management*.

Some elders are unhappy about the use of ideas from sport, commerce and industry being applied to the workings of the Church, because they view them as worldly intrusions which have nothing to do with the work of an elder. The elder's work is spiritual. They feel that by emphasising good manage-

LEADING GOD'S PEOPLE IS NOT ONLY ABOUT THE NATURE OF LEADERSHIP. IT IS ABOUT CARRYING OUT EFFECTIVE LEADERSHIP. WE DO NOT WANT TO BUILD JUST ANY OLD TEAM, BUT ONE WHICH WILL HAVE A CHANCE OF WINNING.

ment procedures we may shut God out of our work.

In Luke 16:1-12 Jesus tells a story of a roguish steward whose rich master suddenly called him to account because he had heard rumours that his property was being squandered. The steward, realising the danger of his situation, set about arranging matters with his master's debtors so that he would have house and home to fall back on when the axe finally fell.

Whilst not approving of the steward's dishonesty, Jesus commended to his followers the vigour, decisiveness and astuteness with which the problem was tackled.

> *As a result the master of this dishonest manager praised him for doing such a shrewd thing; because the people of this world are much more shrewd in handling their affairs than the people who belong to the light.*   Luke 16:8

Here, as in many other places in the Bible, good stewardship is equated with good management. 'Stewardship' means the proper use of talents and resources in God's service. In modern translations the word 'manager' is the usual term given for steward, as in the story above which the *Good News Bible* places under the heading 'The Shrewd Manager'.

In the Gospels, good stewardship is always praised and rewarded; bad stewardship is condemned, as in the story of the three servants in Matthew 25:14-30.

WE CANNOT AVOID THE TASK OF MANAGEMENT.

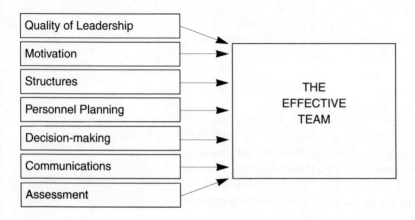

GOOD MANAGEMENT CAN
HELP US TO BE OPEN TO
THE MOVEMENT OF GOD'S
SPIRIT.

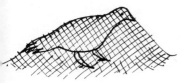

If there is a difference between managing a firm and running a Session, it is a difference of quality rather than function. Leading people into the Kingdom of God is much the more important of the two. And yet people manage corner shops with more dedication and skill than is often brought by Sessions to their work for the Kingdom!

Elders acting together in Session can learn a lot from good management procedures in other organisations. There is nothing in our faith which indicates that we should not try to do so and certainly nothing which says 'Blessed are the inefficient'!

We would wish to argue that far from a concentration on good management procedures preventing the action of God's Spirit, we may, by poor management, exclude God's Spirit from our agenda.

Good management can help us to be open to the movement of God's Spirit.

A successful Session is one that takes time to consider where it is going and how it will get there. Where progress is being made two principles generally arise. The Session is taking a new look at its responsibilities; the Elders are becoming more involved in the planning and execution of policies.

Ian Strachan
'Management in the Kirk Session', *Frontline* B6

By management is meant simply 'how things get done'. The use of management ideas are not necessarily complicated or difficult, as many Sessions are now finding out. Indeed, many elders probably know them already from their everyday lives.

Nor is it a new phenomenon in Sessions, even if it is not always recognised. How many Sessions run on the one-man-band principle where the minister or clerk does everything? How many work on the 'do-nothing' system, maintained by infrequent meetings and a deliberate lack of activity?

The need for management applies both to large

Sessions and to small Sessions. How this is worked out may be different but the principles are the same.

We cannot avoid the task of management. The choice lies between good, productive procedures and poor inefficient ones.

THE CHOICE LIES BETWEEN GOOD AND BAD PROCEDURES.

Quality of leadership

While the whole Session works as a leadership team within the congregation, there are certain key posts within the Session. These are the positions of moderator and clerk.

GOOD LEADERSHIP IS ENABLING LEADERSHIP.

The moderator is important because he/she is in the chair at the Session meeting, and good chairmanship can go far in helping a group to function effectively. Unfortunately ministers may receive little or no training in how to conduct a meeting. As a result, most learn by trial and error how good – or bad – they are.

A Session is required to appoint someone to take its minutes and to keep its records. But the position of clerk can be much more than that of minute-taker. Some holders of this post concentrate on 'doing the paperwork'; others use their knowledge of legal or administrative procedures to 'keep the Session right'. In our team we conceive of the clerk as a kind of chief administrative officer, helping the Session to identify its tasks and ensuring the implementing of its policies.

A good personal relationship between moderator and clerk is vital. They need to be compatible and to know each other. In some places this is helped by the provision of training weekends where both can learn together and share fellowship with each other.

It is also important that this pair see their role in terms of developing and supporting the Session rather than dominating it. The idea of 'enabling' is useful here. These office-bearers are helping the Session to discover its own potential, even if that means allowing some mistakes to happen.

For ministers especially, team management involves a sort of self-denying ordinance, by which responsibility and decision-making are given to the elders as a whole. Thus the ministry of the active Session is liberated in an open and shared way.

The moderator and clerk should act together in a way that reflects the quality of work and relationships in the Session as a body. They have a particular responsibility for creating a 'climate' in which team leadership can flourish. They are 'the team of the team of the team'!

Motivation

It is clearly important that elders are committed to the work of the Session and to their share in it. This will be reflected in the number who attend the Session meetings regularly, carry out their duties in a proper fashion, and actively participate in what is going on. A successful team is one that is highly motivated.

There may be sound reasons why elders do not get involved as fully as they should. Work or domestic commitments may make regular involvement impossible. Many long-serving elders may be unable to undertake duties through age or infirmity. But many more have lost their motivation because nothing of importance ever happens at Session meetings or they are unlikely to contribute anyway.

Some of these difficulties arise from weaknesses in selection. Elders may not know why they are there, what they should be doing – and may not even be interested in doing anything.

People are motivated by different factors and these have to be built into the way our Sessions operate:

1 *Affection:* people need to know they are cared for.
2 *Rewards:* elders have to get something out of their work, such as satisfaction, fun, good feeling, a sense of achievement, success.

3 *Involvement:* elders have to feel themselves to be a part of what is happening, for example, by taking part in discussion, by having their views taken seriously, by doing a specific task.

4 *Control:* elders need to feel that they have some say in what is being decided, rather than that decisions are being made elsewhere, that the same old clique runs everything, that the Session is merely a 'rubber-stamp'.

While love of the Lord should be enough to motivate elders, some skill and effort is required to ground motivation in the needs of people in a practical way. Part of this effort lies in building the kind of teamwork described in chapter 4. Some of it comes from the development of active participation.

The moderator and clerk are crucial in creating the right conditions for real participation. If participation is not just to be an empty gesture, but a motivating force, then certain conditions have to be met.

1 The invitation to participate must be genuine and not just a means of manipulating people.

2 The value of participative methods must be accepted and built into the normal way of doing business.

3 The problems tackled must be worth the time and effort of all concerned. A lot of participation falls down because the issues involved are too small or trivial.

4 The 'contract' must be clear. People should know what they are becoming involved in – for how long, how often, how much effort.

5 The individuals concerned must have the skills and information to enable them to participate effectively. This means training and guaranteed access to whatever is required for doing the job properly.

Various techniques are available to make full use of participation and to provide motivation:

SESSION MATTERS

SESSION MATTERS

The matter of meetings

On a pulpit exchange in Georgia, USA, I ministered one summer to a congregation which had a beautiful white wood church building. One could imagine, in some old movie, Gary Cooper walking by, accompanied by his lady, her parasol for shade in her hand. It was a charming setting.

The church windows had shutters – which were always closed. One Sunday before the service I commented on them. A minute later a rather precocious teenage girl had gone round and opened them all. After the service I asked some of the members why the shutters had always been closed and whether they minded them open. They didn't mind at all. It was so beautiful to have the sunlight coming in, highlighting the colours of the pulpit, pews, carpeting and floors.

Some had no idea why the shutters were always closed. Others explained that one day the sunlight had hit an elderly, now deceased, matron's eyes. She had ordered the shutters closed – and they had remained so until this particular day.

One day I was talking to the Session clerk about why their Session met so rarely. He said, 'Oh well, I suppose that's why so little goes on here'.

How regularly does *your* Session meet and what is the percentage turn-out at your meetings? My former Session used to say that there were only three reasons why someone should not be present at the monthly meeting: work commitments, a parent/teachers meeting, or the fact that one was ill – seriously!

I remember, elsewhere in the States, hearing about a powerful Session whose minister stopped an elder on the Session night at the Session room door, saying: 'What are you doing here?' The elder gave the obvious reply. 'But you have a union meeting this evening,' said the minister. The elder left for his union meeting. Yet another reason for absence?

If your percentage turn-out is causing concern, could the reason in part be because what is on the agenda is often not of gripping consequence? Is it anything to do with how the meeting is structured – where those who don't mind speaking do all the speaking and the more hesitant keep silent, at least at the meeting? Do some of your fellow elders feel it makes no difference whether they are present or not?

I think we have to look at questions like these before we get too annoyed at non-attenders. Thereafter we can tackle with them the question of why they appear to feel that they do not belong.

A MANAGEMENT MODEL
(used in many churches)

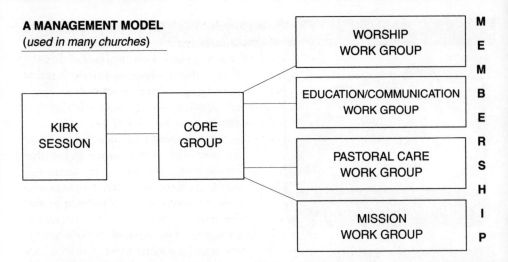

1 Form 4 workgroups (not committees!) These are: **Worship**; **Education**; **Pastoral Care**; **Mission**.

2 Appoint 2 elders to lead each workgroup.

3 All other elders are asked to choose one group to be involved in.

4 Each group is asked to form its own remit (*ie* areas for which it will have responsibility).

5 Each group is then asked to assess their 3 priorities for the coming year.

6 The 2 leaders of each group form the **Core Group** plus the Minister and perhaps an outside consultant. [The core group in our present structure is seen as an executive of **Kirk Session**.]

7 The core group is the clearing house cum think tank for the aims which the individual groups wish to achieve.

8 The core group is given powers from the Kirk Session to agree and progress the aims of the work groups, only needing Session approval if there is a major financial or policy decision to be made.

9 The core group meets every 8 weeks.

10 The work groups meet on week 1 and 7.

11 The core group reports at every Kirk Session meeting on the work of the work groups.

12 Once the aims have been agreed the workgroups can co-opt people from the membership to progress their agendas.

13 In this model not only is leadership efficiency enabled, it is also able to make better decisions because each group has a clear area of operations.

14 This model also enables Kirk Session to delegate effectively thus enabling it to concentrate on the job of management.

15 This model also ensures the entire Session team are always fully informed and better able to make clear policy when planning strategies for the future.

- a Session needs to look at its structures to see to what extent involvement is encouraged;
- the use of small groups, even in the full Session meeting, allows those who feel uncomfortable speaking to a large audience to contribute;
- elders require access to the agenda so that what is discussed reflects their needs and interests;
- a record can be maintained of elders' talents, interests and commitments so that tasks can be allocated appropriately and evenly;
- positions can be rotated regularly to be fair to willing workers and to spread experience and responsibility more widely;
- regular meetings need to be held in both formal and informal settings so that elders get to know each other;
- the seating at meetings can be arranged to encourage involvement, *ie* in a circle or open square rather than in rows;
- Session decisions require to be made only in the Session meeting.

Please recognise that generating motivation takes time and must be constantly reviewed. But it is worth it to release the energy, spirit, expertise and skills which many Sessions contain in their membership.

Structures

Effectiveness depends a good deal on the size of the Session. Obviously a Session which has ten members will work in a different fashion from one with fifty members. Structures need to be devised to suit the numbers and the desired level of participation.

Delegation of business to smaller groups is becoming a more popular feature of many Sessions. The groups can take the form of committees or working parties and can be used for a number of purposes:

- To make use of particular skills and talents.

- To involve more elders in decision-making.
- To gather and process information and ideas.
- To get action carried out.
- To provide links with other bodies and groups.
- To resolve disputes or hold inquiries.
- To encourage the sharing of responsibility.

Such working parties can take a number of forms:

1 standing groups which are formed automatically each year to be concerned with continuing areas of regular activity;
2 ad-hoc groups which are formed on a short-term basis for some specific purpose;
3 representative groups which are appointed to represent the Session in dealings with outsiders.

There are some difficulties for small Sessions in trying to set up working parties, because they feel they have insufficient numbers to do so. One possibility in that situation is the device known in parliamentary terms as 'a committee of the whole House'. This means that the whole Session acts as a working party with the agenda divided up into a series of subject areas. Under each heading the Session is operating as if it were a working party for that sphere of activity.

Another possibility for small Sessions is to appoint elders individually, or in pairs, to look after a particular part of the Session's work, *eg* a Christian education elder (see also page 38, 'The numbers game').

'Committees' often get a bad name because they are seen as time-wasting and inefficient. Where this is the case it is a result of mis-management and a failure to use groups in the best possible way. A number of points have to be borne in mind in forming and developing working parties in the Session.

1 Each active member of the Session should automatically be allocated to a working party. This prevents such work from being seen as the preserve of a limited few or an optional extra in eldership.

2 Working parties should meet often enough to demonstrate they are involved in substantial work.

3 Remits to working parties should be matters of substance, central to the life of the congregation.

4 Working parties should report regularly to the Session and remits should be reviewed periodically.

5 Membership of working parties should rotate, maintaining a balance between the interests of elders and the need for fresh stimulation.

6 Working parties might be allowed to co-opt members of the congregation with specific knowledge of their areas of activity.

7 The choice of conveners is important. It should certainly not always, if ever, be the minister.

8 Wherever possible, some practical outcome to the working parties' deliberations should be encouraged so that talk and action flow from each other.

The basic structure of the Session is most commonly related to districts, *ie* most elders are based in a pastoral unit. There is a case, however, for seeing this as only one possible form of organisation. Some elders might fulfil other leadership functions on the Session rather than that of a district elder. Working party conveners come into this category. By having them concentrate for a given period on this work, certain advantages accrue:

• the working parties are more likely to work;
• skills are more appropriately used;
• time and energy are utilised more fully;
• interest and enthusiasm are properly channelled.

The structuring of time is also important. If working parties are going to function effectively, they have to meet regularly. In some Sessions, where devoting one night a week to being an elder is taken seriously, then attendance at a working party on one evening a month may operate. In other Sessions an alternating system occurs: one month the Session meets in full, the next it meets in its working parties. A third possibility is that the first part of the monthly meeting is held in working parties, then all come together for the remainder of the business.

Personnel planning

Sessions, like all organisations, are composed of people and the effective team has to take into account how people function and how best to make use of the talents and personalities of those who are elders.

Depending upon the structures which exist, it is important to get the right people into the right jobs. There is a two-fold difficulty here: persuading the appropriate person to take on a job, and persuading the wrong person to relinquish a post.

Rota and time limits

The principles of rotation and fixed time-limits have much to commend them in this respect.

Rotation spreads the tasks evenly around the Session, gives many elders a chance to do something and gain experience. It prevents personal empires from being built up.

Fixed time-limits, of say three to five years, help motivation, relieve fears of being landed with a job for life, and provide an honourable means of giving up a post to those who feel tired or inadequate.

These are ideas which are spreading in use: some far-sighted Sessions are even able to arrange for staged transfers of duties and a real system of 'succession'.

Talent spotting

Filling positions involves a keen system of talent-spotting, both inside and outside the Session. It is not necessary for elders to fill all the posts in the congregation, but it is their job to see these posts are filled.

Talent-spotting not only gets jobs done, but involves members of the congregation in the life of the

Elder Trainers

Presbytery elder trainers in the United Free Church, Church of Scotland and Presbyterian Church of Southern Africa can offer three basic courses to elders and interested others:

- 'Being An Elder' – uses *Leading God's People* as its text and explores Faith, the Church, Kirk Session, and the District Elder.
- 'Learning To Care' – uses *Caring for God's People* (the companion to *Leading God's People*) as its text and looks at pastoral visiting, specifically in terms of visiting those in grief and loss, the lapsed, those with a grievance, and pastoral prayer.
- 'Something To Share' – explores faith-sharing and looks at what we have to share and with whom, our faith story, difficult faith questions, discipling, and caring for new Christians.

These well-received courses can be tailored to suit the needs of Presbyteries, local congregations and individual Kirk Sessions and involve discussion and practical exercises as well as the giving of background information.

Church. District elders can play an important role here in identifying the talents and skills available and how best they might be used. It is worth remembering that the goal of stewardship is not just about increasing financial givings. It includes the development and use of people's time and talents. A list of such talents can readily be drawn up using a questionnaire or simply by asking people, where a worthwhile job exists to be done.

In-service training

In making the most effective use of its man- (and increasingly, woman-) power, the importance of training needs to be grasped firmly by the Session. In many occupations in-service training is increasingly seen as vital.

As indicated previously, this may occur at congregational, presbytery and national levels. It can be geared to a wide range of different aspects of the elder's work. Beyond the local Session there are available many training opportunities:

- in talking about the faith;
- in pastoral visiting and care;
- in mission and outreach;
- in the nature of eldership;
- on the meaning of discipleship today;
- for ministers and clerks in Session management.

Within the Session it is possible to build in training opportunities as a regular feature of Session life by:

- alternating training with business meetings;
- having a training period at each meeting;
- establishing annual weekend and day conferences.

Various materials are now available to provide a starting-point for such occasions, both in printed and video form. If we are seeking to improve the preparation of new elders through training, we can hardly expect less from those who are already ordained.

Specialist roles

It is common for Session clerks not to be responsible for a district because of their specialist role as clerks.

It would be surprising to appoint people to be Sunday School Superintendents and Boys' Brigade Captains and not to have them on the Session. To ask them to undertake district work as well could be unfair and detrimental to another aspect of their work.

We might wish to have on Session other 'specialists', for example a Christian local councillor, a head teacher, a youth and community worker to aid the leadership effectiveness of the Session. These people might not have the time to undertake responsible district work. They may indeed lack the expertise for district work, which is itself a 'specialist' task. We have more to say about this on pages 92-93.

Some Sessions have created 'community' elders – elders who do not have a district of members' homes, but who specialise in reaching out to non-members and in encouraging Session to focus on outreach.

Some Sessions have appointed 'industrial' elders who give attention to the working lives of members and the ways in which the congregation can support them. The job could involve:

- encouraging Sessions to be more conscious of work-life problems;
- supporting participation of individual Christians in management, trade unions and professional associations;
- providing a link between the local church and the wider work of industrial mission;
- helping the Session to relate the Gospel to the real issues of industrial life.

In a period when industrial strife and high unemployment are common features of everyday life, an industrial elder can play a significant role in the Church's ministry of reconciliation.

Model for Action
Session agenda

The following model is used as the basis for a printed Agenda which is issued to members before a Session meeting. Comments on the nature of the items are included in brackets.

The Session will meet in the Session room on the third Wednesday of the month at 7.30 pm. The Agenda for the meeting is attached. Any additional items of business should be given to the Clerk before the meeting.

Agenda

Order of the day
Item 7 will be taken before 8.00 pm
(This device allows an item of business of particular importance or involving a visiting speaker or to be taken out of order at a stated time.)

1 *Constitution*
(including opening devotions)

2 *Apologies for absence*

3 *Previous meeting(s) Minutes*
(If possible, printed and circulated with call notice.)

4 *Matters arising*
(Continuing items not dealt with elsewhere.)

5 *Committee reports*
(Including all kinds of working parties and groups.)

6 *Visitations of organisations*
(Reports from visitation elders, phased throughout the year.)

7 *Study/discussion period*
(Allows for Bible study, training, discussion groups, visiting speakers, on regular basis.)

8 *Communion arrangements*
(As necessary.)

9 *Presbytery matters*
(Commissions, reports, meetings with Presbytery delegations.)

10 *Assembly matters*
(Commissions, formal reports, responses to deliverances.)

11 *Correspondence*
(Letters to the Session.)

12 *Other business*
(Admissions; appointments; congregational events; community, national/international issues; especially for matters raised through prior intimation by members.)

13 *Dates of next meetings*
(To be agreed.)

14 *Closure*
(Prayer and benediction.)

Decision-making

Leadership involves taking decisions and in the local church the place where decisions should be made is the Session meeting, though in the United Reformed Church the Church Meeting has an important role also. Elders need to feel that the Session meeting involves real decision-making and not merely 'going through the motions'.

Agenda

The key to an effective team meeting is the agenda. A number of factors relate to successful agenda-making:

1 *Preparation:* Agendas should not simply be allowed to develop on their own momentum. Preparation is necessary, either by the moderator and clerk, or by a small business committee on which members sit by rotation. The purpose is to ensure the business carried out at each meeting reflects the concerns and priorities of the congregation and the demands of the Gospel by which we live.

2 *Use of Time:* Meetings should be held at regular intervals. For an active Session engaged seriously in its leadership tasks, that means monthly. This allows business to be dealt with as it arises. In addition it creates an opportunity for 'capital B' business to occur: fellowship building, consideration of priorities, study and discussion. Agreement on the maximum length of a meeting can also be helpful in concentrating attention and clarifying commitment, though it should not be so rigidly enforced that a meeting is brought to a halt regardless of the importance of the matter in hand.

It can be dangerous to include 'Any Other Competent Business' on the agenda. It can lead to inadequate time being given to a serious matter. It can also be a golden opportunity for those who wish to sabotage the Session. Business worthy of consideration can be brought to the Session's attention at some earlier point for decision as to how and when it will be handled.

3   *Planning:* Within the agenda, items should be planned in advance so that each piece of business is adequately introduced, all know what is going to be discussed, and a wide range of elders can be involved. Having written notice of the business to be transacted several days before the meeting is extremely useful in allowing this to happen.

4   *Interest:* The agenda should reflect matters which concern elders or which have been raised with elders in their districts. Members of Session need to feel that they have access to what goes into the agenda, and that they are free to put forward items for inclusion. This can be done either through the small group preparing the agenda or by giving notice before the meeting.

5   *Balance:* An agenda should contain a good balance of items, providing variety between major issues and formal reporting, debates on general principles and routine matters. It is better not to have too many lengthy debates in the one meeting. Balance should be maintained between meetings as well as within them, *ie* an agenda of major items in one month might be followed by a more routine one the next.

6   *Progression:* Agendas can become very stale with the same business appearing each time in a highly predictable manner. It is necessary that matters are progressed, so that decisions are implemented and the next stage of the policy is attained. For example, a working party having been given a remit, an indication of when its recommendations can be expected might be agreed.

7   *Activity:* Session meetings should be set up in such a way that as many elders as possible are given encouragement and freedom to join in. This can be achieved through:

- planning of reporting arrangements;
- seating arrangements;
- use of group discussions
  ... not always meeting in full Session where some talk a lot and many sit silent throughout.

Control and delegation

To enhance the Session as a decision-making body it is useful to distinguish between control and delegation. Using working parties does not necessarily reduce the responsibility or overall control of the Session. It will still define what the committees do and their recommendations do not become policy until approval is given by the full Session meeting. In this way 'the buck' rests where it ought.

Running a Session meeting so that it takes effective decisions requires considerable skill, but all elders should be aware of the problems that can occur so that they might be avoided.

- Some proposals fail to be considered or to receive proper attention. This is less likely to happen if there are working parties in particular areas and a carefully planned agenda.

- We have already described the situation where everyone nods or stamps approval, but has no real intention of being involved in implementation. It is essential that business be properly discussed and that the precise means of putting the policy into effect be fully agreed.

- Majority decision-making could involve a vote being taken. This is quick and may be efficient if there has been enough time for the item to be

aired. Voting certainly strengthens the commitment of the majority. However it may not win
over the minority unless the Session is a team
where the wishes of the team are seen as more
important than those of an individual.

- Consensus may be false or forced. Silence does
  not mean consent. Forced opinions are of little
  value if members have not actually formed an
  opinion. True consensus comes only when elders
  feel free to express their opinions and are willing
  to keep working together to develop a decision
  that does not necessarily please everyone. This
  depends on a teamwork which allows different
  opinions without bitter disagreement.

- Discussion can become competitive with a number of people trying to make a good impression
  and scoring points over others, rather than really
  contributing to the debate. There may be 'hidden
  agendas' simmering below the surface. The rule
  of one contribution per person on each item can
  be helpful in such circumstances.

- Open discussion may be difficult if elders are not
  clear about what others expect of them. This
  could be helped by the use of a contract clarifying
  the role of the elder.

To aid decision-making, some Sessions make use
of a business committee or moderator's committee.
This group would include both the moderator and
clerk, some other office-holders such as the roll-
keeper or committee conveners, and one or two
elders elected for their experience or knowledge of
the Session.
The kind of matters which the group deals with
will vary depending on the needs of each individual
Session. The following are possibilities:

Model for Action

The Session Handbook

A means of maintaining information-flow within a Session, especially a large one, is to produce at intervals, *eg* annually, a Session handbook with the following:

1 Names, addresses, phone numbers of all elders.

2 Statement of the expectation of eldership (= 'contract').

3 Listing of the areas covered by each elder's districts.

4 Identification of elders with special duties.

5 Membership of Session committees.

6 Rotas for regular duties, depending on frequency of publication.

7 Descriptions of communion duties.

8 Statement of Session policies, as appropriate.

9 Schedule of visitation of congregational organisations.

10 A list of congregational office-holders, organisations and groups, with addresses of leaders or secretaries.

- arranging the agenda for monthly meetings;
- nominating for vacant posts;
- reviewing the structure and size of elders' districts;
- allocating elders to working parties or groups;
- reviewing the Session's working practices;
- identifying new areas of Session initiative.

Communications

A famous management expert once argued that the prime function of a leader is to establish a proper communication system. It is of crucial importance for our leadership team too.

Within the Session

Especially where the Session is a large body, internal communication can make a great difference to improving teamwork and clarifying thinking. In most voluntary bodies any meeting of importance has some paperwork attached to it. For the Session, at least the agenda and minutes of the previous meeting should be printed and circulated. These can help elders in a number of ways:

- to be prepared for the meeting;
- to think things out in advance;
- to provide a sense of continuity;
- to check on past work;
- to keep absent members in touch;
- to provide a referable guide to decisions and to policies.

Where there are sensitive or confidential matters mentioned, these can be dealt with in ways which preserve confidentiality, as happens in other walks of life.

It is interesting that, when ministers and clerks are asked at training courses what they hope to implement when they return to their Sessions, the item most frequently noted is a printed agenda and minutes. It is a small, relatively uncomplicated, yet vital step towards better communication within the Session.

Other papers can also be helpful. A lot of good information reported by diligent Presbytery or visitation elders gets lost because it is reported verbally, when a short, sharp handout could pass the information on more emphatically. Key points could then be highlighted or discussed on the verbal report. A Session handbook is used in some Sessions to provide an annual or biennial summary of administrative and other arrangements.

Within the congregation

It is of great importance that the Session communicates outside its bounds, particularly to the rest of the congregation. The image amongst members of the 'invisible Session' is more widespread than many elders realise.

Most members should know their district elder, but the Session may otherwise only be seen as a body when seated around the communion table. More regular information to the congregation about what the Session is doing, and a feedback of reactions to proposed plans and programmes, can only help to strengthen Church life. This can be done by:

- more reporting of Session matters in congregational newsletters;
- using specific themes for elders to talk about in their district visiting to obtain reactions;
- inviting representatives of congregational organisations to attend Session meetings to discuss their work;
- creative use of internal noticeboards;
- holding congregational meetings on particular issues.

In the United Reformed Church the congregation exercises a considerable say in matters through the Church Meeting, which must be consulted for certain decisions.

SESSION REPRESENTATIVES
TO ORGANISATIONS.

Much of congregational life is found in its organisations and the Session has a duty to encourage and assist their work. This task is formally described as 'oversight'. It is normally executed through a scheme of visitations by elders, individually or in pairs. Visitations should involve:

- a tangible expression of the Session's good wishes to the organisations;
- an assessment of the needs in terms of maintaining the supply of leaders and members;
- an opportunity for any difficulties to be raised;
- an attempt to evaluate what progress is being made towards their purposes.

Visitations are often seen as a chore, but it is important that the Session should demonstrate its concern for organisations and should keep itself informed about what is going on. Visiting elders should obviously be sympathetic to the groups they are visiting. Knowledge of the area of activity being visited is useful. There is also a strong case for some element of continuity in who is appointed to visit over a period of time. Elders sometimes participate in the organisation's planning meetings.

Some Sessions, in carrying out their oversight of congregational organisations, arrange for representatives of the different agencies that work, for example with young people, to attend a Session meeting where they discuss with elders in small groups ways in which help and support can be given. Two-way communication is always better than one-way.

DISTRICT FEED-BACK

Information and reaction from elders' districts can be fed back into the Session in several ways:

- by having district reports at Session meetings;
- by each district elder meeting regularly with the minister solely to discuss the district;
- by involving elders in home communions, baptismal and funeral visits.

Beyond the congregation

Communication with the wider community is important in projecting the local congregation's image as the frontline of Christian witness and work in the area. Part of this involves specific techniques of publicising the existence and activity of the congregation:

- using posters;
- distributing circulars round the doors;
- using the local press;
- imaginative use of outside notice-boards;
- information leaflets in local hotels/guest-houses;
- small communities – producing a parish magazine;
- publicity on local radio for specific events.

But part of it means creating a reputation for involvement with the concerns of the local community and being regarded as the kind of organisation that is approachable, caring and loving. Links might be forged with community councils, the church premises might be a focus for community activity, and representation could be sought on a number of community groups dealing with particular local interests, such as the elderly and the handicapped. In this way communication promotes mission.

Assessment

The whole success of a team depends upon its results. Team management includes checking on how successful the team is and what results it is achieving. This is an area in which Sessions are particularly defensive and reluctant to act.

While it is true that the life in the Spirit is not to be judged in purely material terms, it is necessary to find out how well our spiritual leadership is doing.

Assessment is often and most easily applied to the congregation's financial state where statistical analysis is clear and appropriate. There the task is to respond to the information and work out implications.

'When last did the Kirk Session stand back from its routine ongoing tasks and consciously evaluate what its goals, and the goals of the congregation, should be in the future.'

Assembly Council Report
to the General Assembly
of the Church of Scotland (1990)

In other areas of Session responsibility, it is just as necessary to look objectively at what is happening, or not happening.

- How many persons are on the communion roll?
- How many people joined and left the congregation last year?
- How many non-attenders do you have?
- How does the rate of attendance at communion compare with the numbers on the roll?
- Are Sunday School numbers going up or down?
- What changes are taking place in the area or community where the church is situated?
- What are the implications of these trends for congregational life?

Statistics are often thought useless because they are not acted upon. Yet simple analysis can provide vital background about what exactly is happening, the trends, and how successful the Session is in involving people and maintaining commitment (see p 90).

Statistics do not tell us everything, but they do tell us a lot more than we are often prepared to admit, especially in the Church. They do provide an important element in the Session's task of monitoring the effectiveness of its own leadership.

It is also useful to keep an eye on how well the Session itself is functioning. Assessing the effectiveness of the Session's structure and organisation is often left to the moderator and clerk, or not done at all. It is much better if there is some deliberate mechanism which regularly checks the working arrangements and suggests improvements.

Review group is the name sometimes given to such a mechanism. The group would consist of a number of elders, if possible with one skilled to some degree in management procedures and thus aware of the role of assessment. Assessment can go on regularly, but perhaps every two years this group could be formed for a major review after which it would be disbanded.

The Church of Scotland Department of National Mission have produced a resource booklet, *Towards Tomorrow*, which gives ministers and Kirk Sessions practical help with analysis, vision statements, identifying gifts and reactivating the lapsed.

ILLUSTRATION OF AN ASSESSMENT EXERCISE

Being a member of the church

In this section we are just wanting to get some background information about the members of our church. The following questions are very simple and will only take a moment to answer:

1 *How many years have you been a church member?*
- [ ] less than a year.
- [ ] one to five years.
- [ ] more than five years.

2 *How many years have you been connected with this church?*
- [ ] less than a year.
- [ ] one to five years.
- [ ] more than five years.

3 *Were you previously a member of another community?*
- [ ] yes.
- [ ] no.

4 *Did you become a church member through ...*
- [ ] being brought up in the church?
- [ ] a crisis experience in your life?
- [ ] marriage/or other significant event?
- [ ] the influence of a Christian friend?
- [ ] some form of evangelistic outreach or parish mission?
- [ ] some other way?
  .... (please specify)

5 *What attracted you to this church rather than others?*
- [ ] it was the nearest church.
- [ ] the fellowship attracted me.
- [ ] the preaching attracted me.
- [ ] the worship attracted me.
- [ ] my friends were there.
- [ ] it was my family church.
- [ ] some other reason?
  .... (please specify)

6 *Do you attend church ...*
- [ ] every or most Sundays?
- [ ] once or twice a month?
- [ ] occasionally?
- [ ] seldom?
- [ ] never?

7 *If you are married, does your spouse attend?*
- [ ] yes.   [ ] no.

8 *If you do not attend church regularly, is this because ...*
- [ ] your state of health prevents you?
- [ ] your employment prevents you?
- [ ] family commitments hinder you?
- [ ] you don't find it helpful.
- [ ] some other reason?
  .... (please specify)

[Extract from questionnaire in *Towards Tomorrow*, Church of Scotland Board of National Mission.]

All elders could be given their turn to serve on it.

Together they would review the Session's practices, try to assess how well Session decisions and policies are being carried out, and report to Session, possibly with recommendations. The group could also consult elders individually about their duties, job satisfaction and felt needs.

Whether or not the minister or clerk should be in the group is open to question. They could be very helpful; they could also inhibit real assessment.

Any review procedure needs honesty and sensitivity – two qualities which should not be lacking in a Christian leadership team.

In principle, no policy enacted by the Session should be implemented without some means of assessing its results. By doing this, a Session can learn, adapt and improve its success rate.

THE EFFECTIVE TEAM
(*see page 94*)

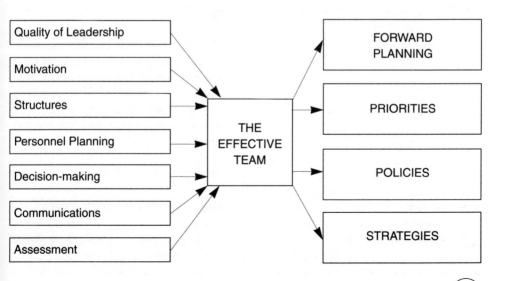

FACTORS IN A PASTORAL STRATEGY

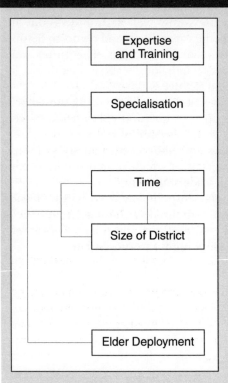

- Expertise and Training
- Specialisation
- Time
- Size of District
- Elder Deployment

Expertise and training

Real pastoral concern requires expertise and spiritual depth if we are to care effectively for those going through the stages of bereavement or facing up to illness, experiencing marital problems and other family difficulties. Developing our gifts and talents in these areas can be greatly helped by the provision of training.

Specialisation

Elders differ, as indeed do ministers, in their ability to relate meaningfully to young couples, senior citizens, lapsed members, non-members. Each of us can tend to be more effective with one or other category. Therefore a Session in working out its pastoral strategy might wish to consider specialisation.

Time

However it is done, if a district is given to you, real pastoral concern requires time. How much time? Should the work output of an elder not be at least as much as that of a Boys' Brigade officer or a Sunday School teacher – *ie* at least one evening a week?

Consider a typical month:

Week 1: evening at Session meeting.

Week 2: evening at Congregational Board meeting.

FACTORS IN A PASTORAL STRATEGY (cont'd)

Week 3: evening in district house group, bringing districts together in fellowship.

Week 4: evening in district.

Some such planned use of time could enable elders to respond, in a way the pre-communion round does not, to events, happy and sad, in the lives of our members. *Real pastoral concern requires time.*

Size of district

Assuming that we are talking about real pastoral concern and not just the delivering of communion cards, then the size of an elder's district is an important factor.

- Does it include the lapsed?
- Does it include any families on the baptismal roll?
- Does it include any houses of non-members?
- How many calls can an individual elder be expected to cope with meaningfully?

Will this not vary from person to person and from the same person from time to time? If so, this will require a strategy which permits flexibility.

Elder deployment

If we think of one evening per week being devoted to one's eldership, it raises the question of the other jobs often given to elders – sometimes to their cost or their families' cost – and to the detriment of their pastoral work.

A decision may have to be made between some of these other jobs and the pastoral task. Often the Session clerk and treasurer do not have district duties. Perhaps others, too, should not have any district duties.

The error of appointing elders on a purely pastoral coverage factor was pointed out on page 44. We may wish to appoint as elders, people with skills in other leadership tasks, people who may not have the time or expertise to fulfil the pastoral role.

Elders are not too easy to find, and certainly not if our standards are above the 'any elder is better than no elder' death wish. When trying to develop an effective pastoral strategy we might therefore wish to consider the use of non-elder visitors, working under the supervision of the Session.

As the pastoral role is not to be seen as purely the minister's, so it may not be the exclusive role of the Session members, though it is their collective responsibility to ensure the best pastoral coverage they can effect.

If we were managers in the commercial world we would be considering these important factors, and we would be working out tactics to cope with the different issues.

The effective team

All of these elements together go to produce the effective team. They have to be worked on. They require patience and perseverance to develop. They need a degree of skill and knowledge to achieve success. Managing the leadership team which is the Session, is no soft option. The characteristics of a well-managed team show themselves clearly in how an effective Session operates.

The effective team plans ahead:

It will want to ask the question, 'Where does God want us now to go?' It takes steps into the future. It takes stock regularly of what has already been achieved and what requires still to be done.

The effective team sets priorities:

It will want to ask the question, 'What is important to establishing God's Kingdom?' It is able to tell the difference between 'small b' business and 'capital B' business. It will allocate its energies and resources to the right issues.

The effective team works out policies:

It will want to ask the question, 'What is it God wants us to do?' It has something to say on topics which matter to people. It takes up a worked-out position on different areas of the Church's life.

The effective team implements strategies:

It will want to ask the question, 'What course of action does God require us to take?' It provides an overall framework for various activities by individuals and groups. It develops processes and procedures to achieve its leadership goals.

Team management, geared towards appropriate goals, is undoubtedly the key to making each congregation the 'frontline' of Christian work and witness.

TEAM MANAGEMENT, GEARED TOWARDS THE APPROPRIATE GOALS, IS UNDOUBTEDLY THE KEY TO MAKING EACH CONGREGATION THE 'FRONTLINE' OF CHRISTIAN WORK AND WITNESS, LED BY ITS SESSION.

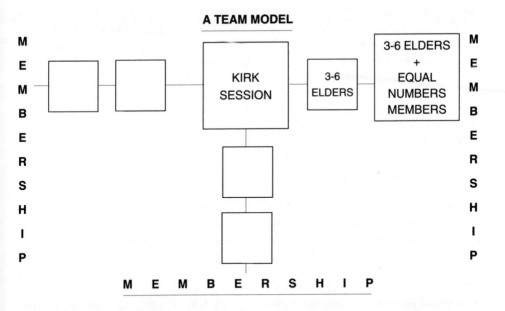

Team Model (above)

1 Assess the gifts/talents of your Kirk Session.

2 Build teams of 3-6 elders (using their talents).

3 A convener is appointed for a fixed term.

4 Assign the elders to an area (possibly 3-6 old districts).

5 Look at membership – see who could be invited to join the team (based on talents required).

6 The original team can be doubled in size.

Advantages of this Model

1 Members can be visited more frequently (thus getting away from the pre-Communion visit).

2 Different expectations of visit.

3 Elders and others can be ministered to and encouraged in their team.

4 At Kirk Session each team convener reports. Therefore in a relatively short space of time any actions required can be noted.

5 Better communication on *all* levels.

6 Apprenticeship system for future possible elders.

ELDERSHIP AND SPIRITUAL GIFTING

A System of Team Ministry

A congregation founded in 1662 has followed closely the traditions of Eldership seemingly embedded in concrete in our National Presbyterian heritage. Increasingly that heritage has developed in a narrowly pastoral style of eldership over against a biblical leadership model. Thus for pastoral oversight our congregational life is in microcosm what our national church pattern is in macrocosm – *ie* a church for every parish (by definition a minister for every parish), therefore an elder in every district. So every elder gets a district to shepherd, but does every elder have pastoral gifts?

Is it without any significance that as the numerical membership of our National Church has declined, the only consistently high figure has been the number of elders ordained?

A superficial assessment of our inherited pattern discovered very quickly that not all elders had pastoral gifts. They were good people, people of faith in God, sincere people, but often people who were 'square pegs in round holes'.

Furthermore, we began to see that elders were not simply to be pastors, but spiritual leaders, those who in a spirit of unified vulnerable love had the supreme function of discerning prayerfully what the Spirit of God is saying in the Church, testing it, processing it and then sharing it with the wider fellowship. While being utterly committed to the principles of democracy in secular life, it has become apparent that this is not a biblical model of Church government. But how does one change an inherited model that in a stable rural setting seemed to have worked to some effect?

Going back to scratch was not a viable option – too many people would be inevitably hurt, the unity of the Church would be in disarray and the glory of the Lord Jesus would be scarred. A prayerful, teaching, consultative process had to be initiated. A number of principles had to be held together:

(a) what the bible says about ecclesiastical leadership;

(b) a loving concern for the pastoral care of the congregation;

(c) commitment to evangelism in the parish.

The broad cradle for this is an understanding of, and commitment to, the ministry of the whole body. Every believer is spiritually gifted and, within this, there are those gifted with visionary leadership, as there are those with pastoral skills.

So a system of Team Ministry has grown over the years covering the whole range of the work of an ordinary congregation. The Kirk Session took a primary role in deliberation and decision. Every current elder made a commitment to membership of at least one ministry team as

ELDERSHIP AND SPIRITUAL GIFTING (cont'd)

they felt themselves gifted or skilled. These teams were then extended to include up to 200 members of the wider congregation on the same basis. Crucial to this is the fact that the convener of each team is an elder, so that the whole structure is rooted in and overseen by the Kirk Session.

When electing elders now, we do this strictly adhering to the principles of Church Law. We nominate, elect and ordain only when we are satisfied prayerfully that the person senses both a call and has leadership gifts. This has meant a revue of our Pastoral Care system. Our district system has been re-vamped. Homes in the congregation have been regrouped into units of about six, with one home being responsible for the other five.

The process is simple. Instead of the former, usually quarterly, visit by an elder, who often lived outwith his district, there is now to be weekly contact by the designated people to the other five homes, simply to keep up-to-date with any developments.

To this end, the telephone, a passing conversation in the garden, or, if required, a knock on the door, is adequate. Maybe the weekly contact might even be in Church on Sunday! A situation that is then requiring attention is passed to our Care Ministry Team in conjunction with the Pastoral staff (usually the Minister) who follow up quickly. Needless to say, current or future elders, if they wished, would be part of this whole system, either as contact homes or in pastoral care response.

Is it working?
We cannot be sure yet, but we do not believe it is too revolutionary to work.

Can it work anywhere?
Absolutely, and it can be improved upon.

The advantages of this are clear:

(a) Spiritual leadership becomes the major concern of the Kirk Session;

(b) Elders need only be appointed when the Spirit leads – and the Kirk Session, clearly, has no need to be the unwieldy size it so often is in many churches;

(c) Elders are still appointed prayerfully within the constitution of the Church of Scotland;

(d) Spiritual gifts are then able to be effectively used within a wider team situation;

(e) Pastoral care of the congregation becomes more immediate and widespread;

(f) The Body of Christ is built up.

6

GAINING GROUND

'Yes,' say elders to us on training courses throughout the land, 'we want to carry out our duties better and more efficiently, *but ....* '

The creation of a Session as a leadership team, able to achieve its goals, does come up against all sorts of problems, as outlined in chapter 3.

Part of good management is handling problems. We believe that the development of teamwork and the use of sound management procedures are important to making progress and gaining ground. Dealing with problems can be compared to the way in which a doctor tackles an illness. There are four parts to this:

1 *Diagnosing the problem*

This stage includes:

- being clear about your own goals and purposes;
- knowing what is important and what is not;
- recognising what can be resolved and what cannot.

It is vital to distinguish between the 'symptoms' and the 'disease', to make the difference between the surface problems (the symptoms) and the real problems (the disease). If an elder has not attended a Session meeting for the past year without good reason, absenteeism is obviously a 'symptom' of something, but closer inquiry is needed to find the real 'disease'.

2 *Deciding on the treatment*

This stage involves choosing an appropriate course

of action to deal with the problem. Change is probably required in one or more of the following areas:

- *people:* by reallocating, training or giving help;
- *structures:* by looking again at how jobs are done or by relating people to each other in different ways;
- *procedures:* by adjusting the systems used for communicating, motivating, passing on information, and making decisions.

A danger here is to seek the completely right solution and to do nothing until we find it. Another danger is not to take enough time to work out a solution. Sessions often rush into activity before knowing exactly what it is they are going to do.

ILLNESS   **HEALTH**

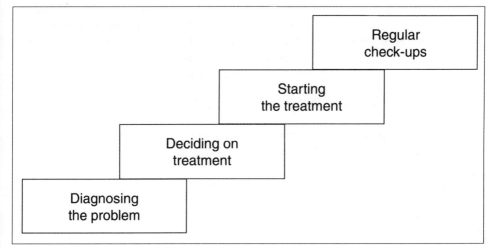

3 *Starting the treatment*

This stage involves getting something done to begin to improve the condition. This requires:

- creating an awareness of a need for change;
- using the proper means of getting things going;
- involving people.

It is important that once a course of action has been agreed by the Session, some activity, no matter how small, should begin. In this way elders can see that the decision taken will be put into practice.

4 *Regular check-ups*

After an illness good personal health depends on regular check-ups. Session teamwork requires the same. This involves:

- *comparing results with intentions:* how did our policies actually work out?
- *obtaining feedback:* what information comes back to us from other people?
- *continuous modification:* as no plan is ever perfect, what small adjustments are needed?

In these four stages it is necessary to bear in mind that:

- *how* things *happen* is as important as *what* happens;
- *how* people *feel* is as important as *what* is achieved.

It should be noted too that handling problems and gaining ground always involve choices:

- choices about *what* to do;
- choices about *how* to do it;
- choices about *when* to do it;
- choices about *who* will do it.

Gaining ground is also about change. Just as the movement from illness to health requires alteration and adjustment, so Christian leadership involves the Session in adapting to and indeed encouraging change. As we said in chapter 3, change is coming at us in the Church from various directions and we do tend to be resistant to it.

Change for its own sake is of little or no value.

But it is clear that we require to accept some change if Sessions are to develop their teamwork and leadership capacity.

Successful adaptation to coping with change can be encouraged in the following ways, which together form a cyclical pattern.

(a) *Sensing the need for change:* this is based on having a sensitive 'intelligence' network. It may occur when new elders are admitted to the Session, bringing with them a new awareness. Or when a new minister arrives, or a new appointment is made to a key post. This again is a good reason for rotation of jobs.

One or two individual elders may become conscious that some improvement could be made. This might happen through a conversation in a district household, or by speaking with elders in other Sessions, or by learning new ideas at a training course.

Where a Session engages itself in regular self-assessment, then the need for change can emerge from that.

(b) *Importing the relevant information to where it can be acted upon:* awareness of the need for change has to be brought into the whole Session system. This may mean presenting a report which contains the facts at a meeting. It may involve setting up a working party to look into the matter, ensuring that it is representative of the range of views within the Session.

Suggestions have a better chance of success if they have the support of the Session 'opinion-leaders', the elders whose lead others will follow.

An outside party can be of value in helping Sessions come to terms with new ideas, perhaps in the context of a training conference or a talk by a visiting speaker. The main purpose here is to create an awareness that will lead to action.

(c) *Altering the process or procedures according to the information:* this means actually making the relevant change. It involves getting general agreement to do something which alters the methods or structures by which activities are already carried out. Such consensus is a common outcome in a Session that has developed teamwork, as described in chapter 4.

(d) *Stabilising these internal changes, while reducing or managing any undesired by-product:* it is not enough just to make a change – it has to be fixed into the system. This might mean agreeing to allow a new procedure to operate for a trial period. Or making a new activity, such as a Session study period, a fixed item on the agenda at each meeting.

It also involves watching out for unintended consequences. It is not the first time that a plan designed to increase elder participation actually has led to fewer elders participating! Or a change that solves a problem in one sphere of the Session's work produces new problems in a completely different sphere.

(e) *Running the new system:* change has got to be given time to work. Having agreed to implement a change, it must be allowed to operate fully so that its effects can be properly judged. Perhaps in the Church we tend to set new ideas up in such a way that they have little chance of succeeding, especially by giving them insufficient time and support in which to take root.

(f) *Obtaining feedback and checking results:* find out what the consequences of the change have been. This might be done through: quantitative checks, *ie* any measurable ways of assessing results; checks on attitudes or feelings, for example, by the use of questionnaires or opportunities for opinion-gathering; behavioural checks, *ie* how people's actual behaviour is different from before.

This process is cyclical in nature as the diagram below illustrates. The last stage becomes a basis for the first stage to feed upon and so the momentum is maintained.

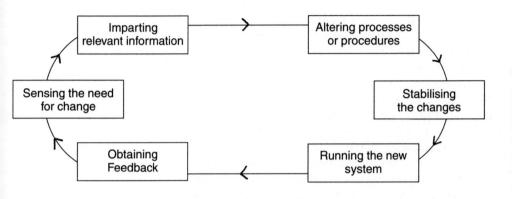

Discipline

It is important to enable elders to see what is happening, or not happening, and why this is the case, even if it means confronting them with their own actions and the consequences of those actions.

No team can play as well as it can and have a chance of winning if half the players are sitting in the dressing room, pleased to wear the team colours, but not prepared to go out on to the field of play. They have either to play the game or hang up their boots.

If we were playing for the World Cup we would know this. It must be even more true for a Session team which is playing for something infinitely more important than the World Cup! *Session discipline is therefore essential.*

In a Christian team the exercise of discipline should always be carried out in a way which makes it clear that love and compassion are at its core. But there may be occasions when it requires to be done.

Every encouragement must be given to Session members to play their part. Remember what was said on page 59 about being fair to those who came into the team on an inadequate contract.

Good management must be exercised, but the point may come when a 'non-player' has to be removed for the good of the team, and, more importantly, for the overall goal which we are trying to achieve. Indeed for some, this might come as a welcome relief.

Gaining ground –
by facing the challenge of the Gospel

We can look back to the Victorians and the Edwardians and give thanks for their contribution to the life of the Church: *eg*, for the Boys' Brigade, Sunday School, Woman's Guild, the Choir and many of the hymns we still sing. For what will future generations be able to thank us?

It would be good if they could thank us for the faithfulness that helped God bring about the renewal of the local congregations as the frontline in Christian education and mission; congregations that are truly Christian resource centres where discipleship is encouraged, real Christian fellowship provided, and Christians given the confidence and desire to share their faith with the world.

If this is to happen the role of the elder, and in particular the collective role of the Session, is quite crucial. We have to be not just 'pillars' of the Church, but 'propellers', leading God's people to a new understanding of their shared ministry. If we can achieve this, future generations will be able to give thanks.

We hope that this book has presented you with something of the excitement and challenge of the eldership and that you feel encouraged to develop, with your fellow elders, a dynamic leadership team in your congregation. In the final chapter there is a lot of material for team discussion.

Together we must face up to the problems in these changing times for our society and for the Church. Together, in Christ, we must manage our leadership task in ways that reflect our faith in a God, not only of yesterday, but of today, and of tomorrow.

The Bible calls us on page after page to see ourselves as God's pilgrim people, a people on the move:

— *a people who like Abraham, in trust and obedience, are prepared to leave their settled life for the adventure of the open road.*

Hebrews 11:8-9

— *a people who are not afraid of the text, 'I make all things new'.*

Revelation 21:5
see also 2 Corinthians 5:17

— *a people who like Paul know that they have not yet arrived but who press forwards towards the goal.*

Philippians 3:12-13

— *a people who have as their motto, 'We shall become'.*

Ephesians 4:12-13

— *a people who are prepared to answer Jesus' call to 'follow me' and who encourage others to 'come and see'.*

John 1:35-51

Like Moses (Exodus 3) we may find many excuses for avoiding God's challenge to provide the necessary leadership of His people. But Moses responded positively and so must we, and when the people we lead seek to give up the journey, let us, like Moses (Exodus 14:15), encourage them to put their trust in God and go forward.

7

FOR TEAM DISCUSSION

The following material is intended for selection and building into programmes that will help your Session develop its teamwork and leadership potential.

1 *Baseline thinking* (pp 1-20)

Jesus

- Divide into groups of 6 people.
  Divide the groups into A groups and B groups.
    A groups: study Luke 19:1-10.
    B groups: study John 5:1-14.
  Discuss how Jesus, step by step, dealt with
  (A) Zacchaeus and (B) the man at the pool.
  Bring groups together.

  Discuss: What was the effect of Jesus on each man?
  What did it require of each man to bring this about?

- Consider individually:
  If on a pastoral visit you were asked what Jesus means to you, what would you say?
  Share your answers.
  Prepare a group answer.
  Consider what is said about Jesus and the wall/mirror diagram on pages 2-3.
  Bring groups together.
  Share your group answers and your response to what is said about Jesus on pages 2 and 4.

Christianity

- Create a worksheet with the following texts written out in full. Issue a copy to each member of the Session.

    Hebrews 1:1-3
    John 3:16-17
    Galatians 4:4-5
    Ephesians 1:10
    John 8:35; 10:10; 5:11
    Ephesians 4:13, 23-24

Individually, underline anything which you find particularly exciting, challenging, meaningful, difficult. In small groups, share your underlinings and listen to each other.

Discuss:
(a) If on a pastoral visit someone were to ask you what Christianity is about, what would you say?
(b) If on a pastoral visit someone were to describe himself as a Christian not because he knew anything about Jesus, but because he believed himself to be a 'good' person, knowing him to be a 'good' man, what would you say?

Bring groups together to share their answers to these questions.

Church (pp 2-4)

- Divide into groups of three, if possible with members of Session less well-known to each other.
  Share with each other a particularly happy, meaningful church experience you have had at any time in your life.
  Join up groups of three into groups of six. Discuss together when your Church membership became something real for each of you.

- Individually fill in the following:

> **What do you feel about belonging to the Church?**
>
> **Tick any of the following which strike a chord with you:** fun ❏
> responsibility ❏   privilege ❏
> frustration ❏   burden ❏
> treasure ❏ excitement ❏
> disappointment ❏   joy ❏
> challenge ❏   security ❏
>
> **Add any word of your own.**

In small groups, share your responses and the *why* of any response you feel free to share.

- Create a worksheet with the following texts written out in full:

Mark 1:16–18
Mark 3:31–35
Matthew 5:13–16
Matthew 28:18–20
Hebrews 10:24–25
1 Peter 4:8
Ephesians 4:27–32
1 John 1:7
Ephesians 4:22–32
1 Peter 2:9–10

Individually, underline anything which you find particularly exciting, challenging, meaningful, or difficult.
Share your underlinings and listen to each other.
As a group, choose two words which for you express the purpose of the Church.
Bring groups together.
Share your findings. What two words express your Session's understanding of the purpose of the Church?

• In small groups:
Consider quotations on pp 4–7.
Bring groups together.
Share your findings and discuss the concept of shared ministry outlined on pp 6–7.

Eldership (pp 7–19)

• The box on the left can also be used to express what you feel about your eldership. Or the diagrams on page 109 (top right) can be used. The triangle represents your eldership.

Do this individually, then in small groups share your responses and the why of any response you feel free to share.

• In small groups:
Study together Acts 20:17–38.
Consider the material on pp 15–17.
Consider the diagram on p 21.
Do you agree that the role of an elder is to be seen today primarily in terms of leadership and belonging to the leadership body of the congregation?
Bring groups together to share their findings.

• In small groups:
Share together what you remember about your ordination and what ordination means to you.
Discuss the ordination vows of the different denominations mentioned on page 14.
If your group were to be asked to frame a set of ordination vows what would they be?
Bring groups together to share their findings and frame the vows you considers appropriate.

• Consider together:
What are you doing as a Session to help your congregation grow in ministry?
In small groups consider the manifesto. Begin to formulate your own.
Bring groups together and develop a manifesto for your own Session.

A Session manifesto

The following statement was composed by one particular Session as a Charter to express its thinking and intentions. It first appeared in the Report of the Church of Scotland's Committee of 40 in 1976.

(a) The concern of the Session is *people*.

(b) The attention of the Session must be directed to people and their needs; not to 'things' and their maintenance.

(c) The Session must learn 'to listen' to others and to itself and bring a 'new attitude' to hearing reports.

(d) The elder's district is a prime area of involvement. There must be a radically new 'district emphasis' running through *all* our work.

(e) Involvement must be 'involvement in' something, not involvement 'by' serving on a committee.

(f) There must be formal/informal patterns on our routine meetings. We must talk more with each other and not at each other.

(g) We must embark on self-education about our Faith and about the world we live in.

(h) We must attend to big issues and the smaller ones will look after themselves.

2 *Leadership* (pp 21-44)

- In small groups:
  Discuss the idea of the 'outpost' on page 22 and the idea of the 'Christian resource centre' on page 23.
  Consider the diagram on page 23. Are these the leadership goals for a modern Session?
  Is there anything you would wish to add or subtract?
  Bring groups together to share their findings.
  Construct your own leadership goals diagram.

Christian education (pp 24-26)

- Form small groups – consider the following questions as individuals:

  Someone says to you that the Book of Jonah is surely a load of rubbish. What would you say in reply?

  Someone asks you what the Apostles' Creed means by the strange words,

'He descended into hell'. What answer could you give?

Someone asks you to explain what you believe your faith says to you about abortion (or euthanasia or genetic engineering). How would you answer?

A 17-year old who has become interested in the faith asks you to recommend a good, but not too difficult book about the Bible. What would you recommend?

Share your responses.
List the theological or faith questions raised by the common experience of life.
List any particular questions being raised by our modern society.
Note where in the life of the congregation you lead, people are:
(a) allowed to talk about the faith;
(b) encouraged to wrestle with the questions you have listed;
(c) helped to grow in their spirituality.
How is discipleship encouraged in your own Session?

Take it – but don't unwrap it!

Bring groups together to share their findings.

Consider also the slogan on page 24.

• In small groups, consider the following questions:

Your congregation provides a Sunday school and some youth programmes, but what does it do to help the parents fulfil their vows at baptism?

People are given leadership roles in the life of the congregation (like Sunday school teachers, youth leaders, finance committee members, *etc*). What training is there in the life of the congregation to help them?

Many of your members work as solitary Christians at their employment where they are often faced by difficult moral decisions. How are they supported for their witness in the world?

Imagine a 35-year old couple – husband and wife – with plenty of work and leisure interests. They begin to be interested in the Christian faith. In the life of your congregation, what can they take part in *together* which will help to nurture their young faith and support them as they seek to grow?

Consider the model on page 25. In the light of it, what would you wish to develop in your congregation?

What steps might you take to develop what you offer in the way of adult Christian education?

Bring the groups together to share their findings.

- Meet with your Sunday school teachers and your youth leaders to seek to understand their work and how your Session might provide adequate support in the areas of child and youth education.

- Consider: what is your financial budget for the work of Christian education?
  How well is your congregation equipped for the Christian education of all ages in terms of leaders and teaching resources.

Christian fellowship (pp 27-28)

- In small groups: Ask group members to share any experience they have had which they would describe as 'Christian fellowship'.

Christian Education – For All of Life

Define what you understand by 'Christian fellowship'.
What kind of things must be done in a group to help it experience Christian fellowship?

Consider the following:
It is often said that within the life of a congregation there are many meetings but little real meeting.

To occupy the same geographical space, to exchange chit-chat, to listen to speakers, to express opinions, to share a piece of work – these things can lead, as a by-product, to meeting; but they can also, and frequently do, impede real meeting and leave people's need for recognition and understanding, for support and a sense of belonging, largely unattended.

Stewart Matthew
'Thinking about ... the House Church',
Frontline A4

Where can 'real meeting', *ie* Christian fellowship, be experienced in the life of the congregation you lead? How is it fostered in your Session? Is there any relationship between your answers to the last two questions?

Bring groups together to share their findings.

- In small groups:
How is a stranger, or an infrequent attender, at your Sunday services made to feel welcome?
Consider the 'Welcome Duty' model on page 28. Are there any new initiatives you might take?
To increase fellowship are there ways your elders and members could participate more in the conduct of your collective worship? Bring groups together to share their findings and to consider new initiatives.

- In small groups, consider the following:

One of the weaknesses of the Church today is that too many members are trying to cope with life, equipped only with a child's knowledge and understanding of the Christian faith.

It should be one of the main concerns of the minister and kirk session to find ways and means of gathering people together in small groups to explore more deeply the implications of the Gospel for our society and for our individual lives.

People need opportunities of raising their doubts and airing their difficulties, and then sharing the help they have found. Such fellowship is possible only in an informal and intimate small group.

We His Servants

The House Church is a small, face to face group which seeks to be the church of Jesus Christ for its members, more intensively than is possible in larger groupings. The House Church lives the Good News of the Gospel, that all persons are children of God – loveable, worthwhile, equal, acceptable and responsible. Experiencing the Good News liberates us from our bondage to the past. The unfinished business of bygone days – guilt, anger, hurt, pain, grief, injunctions from parents and other authority figures which are no longer operative today, but hold us captive – is overcome through experiencing the love of God and the love of neighbour mediated by house church members.

Philip A Anderson
The House Church

Let group members share any experience they have had of house groups.

What made these experiences good or bad?

Love binds everything together!

- Consider together the following comments:

There is another way in which the Elder can bring his members into the fellowship of the church – by letting them experience it together. So much is said in Church about the wonder of Christian fellowship, all of which is true. But so much of it is wide of the mark because the ordinary member seldom has an opportunity of experiencing it. The truth is that you can't have a real sense of fellowship between a thousand communicants – or even 500. But you have a far greater chance in a group of 20 or 30. And that is where the Elder's district is vital.

G D Wilkie, *The Eldership Today*

George Wilkie emphasises the value of house groups at the heart of congregational life. The elder's district, he says, presents an opportunity for gathering members together in fellowship groups 'which will not cut them off from the larger congregation, but will make (their) activities more meaningful.

Do you agree with this?

What could be done in your congregation to move in this direction?

The publications by S H Mayor and D F Wright (referred to on page 19) stress the importance of the elder's district and its potential for fellowship, as well as the individual care of the elder. Naturally this is easier to develop if the district is a compact geographical area where members' homes are close to each other. If this is not the case, the elder's house or church hall or lounge could be used. Transport can be arranged for those who need it.

Pastoral care (pp 28-30)

- In small groups, consider the following:

Your Session operates some kind of a pastoral strategy, which may or may not have been clearly thought out.

1 What is that strategy?

2 What factors have been taken into account?

3 What elements of the 'Care Visitors' scheme (Appendix 1, p 125) commend themselves to you?

4 In what ways would you wish to

develop your own Session's pastoral strategy?

Bring groups together to share their findings, to consider possible developments and how they might be effected.

• What structures do you have, or could you as a Session develop, to care for each other, including the minister?

GOD'S CONVERSATION
WITH HIS CHURCH
IS ALWAYS ABOUT HIS WORLD.

A LIVELY CHRISTIAN
CANNOT KEEP SILENCE.

Evangelism (pp 30 and 32)

• In small groups:
Recall the wall/mirror diagram on pp 2-3.
List the ways your congregation tries to fulfil its calling to be a blessing to those outside the faith by helping them to share our faith.

Consider:

The pulpit seldom speaks to the world. The world is just not there to listen. The message must be got across in all its boldness, openness and plainness by the laity, the people of God, who are in the world, who live and work and earn their bread there.   Albert Winn

Where, in the life of the congregation you lead, are your members encouraged to talk about their faith meaningfully in relationship to their life 'in the world'?

Is there any relationship between the educational and fellowship provision in your congregation and the congregation's efforts at evangelism?

Bring groups together to share findings and consider development in this regard.

• In small groups:
Study the missionary strategies on pages 32-33. Consider what strategies you might be able to develop in your situation.

Service (pp 32-34)

- Establish three working parties to consider the following:

It dawned on me with a sudden jolt that real prayer, christian prayer, inevitably drives a man, sooner or later, out of the privacy of his own soul, beyond the circle of his little group of Christian friends and across the barriers between social, racial and economic strata to find the wholeness, the real closeness of Christ in that involvement with the lives of the lost and groping children, whoever and whatever they may be.

Keith Miller
The Taste of New Wine

Then tackle the following:

First working party
Research the ways in which your congregation gives active Christian service to the society around it.

Second working party
Research the amount of money the congregation has given in the past twelve months to support Christian service and other social concerns.

Third working party
Identify and research any special needs in the community. Consider how your congregation might help.

Each working party should prepare a written report and have it distributed to all members of Session.
Once the above has been done, have Session meet in small groups with a member of each working party in each group.
Assess the level of Christian services given by your congregation.
Consider any further service you might as a congregation be able to give.

Bring groups together to share their findings.

- In small groups:
Consider any wider national and international issues you feel your Session and congregation should be involved in.
How might this involvement be prepared for and come about?

Bring groups together and share your findings.

Wider links (pp 34-37)

- Establish three working parties to consider the following:

First working party
How could you develop your links with your Presbytery and General Assembly and its departments?
How do you communicate this wider work to your congregation?

Second working party
How could you develop your links with neighbouring Presbyterian Congregations?

Third working party
Recall the wall/mirror diagram on pages 2-3.
How could you develop your relationship with the congregations of other denominations in your area?
Each working party should prepare a written report and have it distributed to all members of Session.

Once the above has been done, have Session meet in small groups with a member of each working party in each group.
How might these matters be forwarded?

Bring groups together to consider what steps you might take in any of these directions.

Maintenance (pp 35-37)

• Create research groups of up to 6 people to carry out the following tasks, one task per group:

(a) Review the congregational roll over the past five years in terms of numbers, genders, age bands. Compare it with the population changes in your area over the same period.

(b) Review the involvement of children and teenagers in the life of your congregation over the past five years. Compare what has been happening to the local school rolls.

(c) Undertake the assessment exercise on page 90 regarding adult involvement in the lifestyle of your congregation and consider it in the light of understanding of shared ministry on page 6.

(d) Review the agendas of your Session over the past five years and list the apparent priorities of your Session.

Have each research group project what the next five years are likely to produce in each regard if there is no change in Session policy. Each research group should prepare a written report of its findings for circulation to all members of Session.

Arrange a Session conference.

Divide members into the four areas of research, according to the interest of each member.

Consider the reports and the implications for the future work of the Session and the possible need for new management structures.

- In small groups, consider the standard of membership your Session apparently finds acceptable.

    Look again at the vows of membership. In the light of these and what is said on page 6 about the shared responsibility for ministry, consider any recommendations you would wish to make to Session.

    Bring groups together to share their thoughts.

Initiative and reaction (pp 37-40)

- In small groups, list likely reasons for a Session's lifestyle being:
    dull;
    unexciting;
    inactive.

    What are the necessary factors for a Session to be:
    lively;
    exciting;
    creative?

    Bring groups together to share their findings and what might be done by your Session to eliminate any negatives and accentuate positives.

    Consider the work of your Session in the light of the Assembly deliverances noted on pages 40-43.

3 *Common problems* (pp 45-51)

- In small groups – discuss (with sensitivity!) whether or not your Session suffers from any of the problems outlined on page 45.

    Consider the numbered paragraphs on pp 46-47:
    Are any of these real problem areas for your Session?

    Consider the matters raised under the heading of 'The problem of change' (p 47).
    Are any of the changes particularly relevant in your situation?
    Is lack of confidence a problem?

    Bring groups together to share their conclusions.
    What might God be asking you to do as a Session to tackle the problem of lack of confidence?

4 *Teamwork* (pp 52-66)

- In small groups discuss whether or not you agree with what is said about the importance of teamwork. Do you agree with the idea of the Session as the leadership '*team* of the team' (page 66)?

    Consider the 'Essentials of Teamwork' diagram on page 54.

    Is there anything you would wish to add or subtract?

Consider which areas of teamwork your Session tackles well and identify areas requiring attention.

Bring groups together to share any findings and to agree any 'Essentials' requiring attention.

- Have each group consider the following 'Essentials' or create groups to tackle one each. Either way, each group should prepare a report for the Session.

Selection procedure (pp 53-59)

- Work out, step by step, how your Session arrives at its decision to approach a person to become an elder.
  Does the attitude 'any elder is better than no elder' play a part in your decisions?
  What are your governing factors?
  How many 'players' does an active session require?

Consider the merits and demerits of Session selecting without reference to the congregation, and those of having the congregation involved in the selection.

Consider the Model for Action (pp 57-58; and what is said on pp 56 and 59.

Consider how you might improve, if necessary, your own selection procedure.

Preparation procedure (pp 53 and 55)

- How were you prepared to become an elder?
  Do you feel what was done for you was adequate?
  What preparation programme does your Session offer to help a person come to his/her decision about your request, with as much understanding as possible of what eldership means and involves?

If your Session does not offer much more than a 'chat with the minister', devise a more adequate procedure. What do you wish to see included in a preparation programme?
Who should take part in conducting the programme?

Contract (p 59)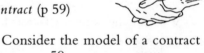

- Consider the model of a contract on page 59.
  What do you feel about the idea of a contract?
  Draw up a suggested contract for your situation.

Take into account the following:

(a) Should regular in-service training be part of the contract?

(b) Some believe that an elder should serve for a fixed period, possibly renewable, with or without a break. This practice occurs in the United Reformed Church.

A different viewpoint is presented in *Session Matters* ('Once An Elder') article on page 65.
What do you feel about this?

(c) In the light of what is said on page 59, what do you feel about providing regular opportunities for elders to re-contract themselves, renew their vows, or be helped to withdraw with dignity if a Session is now operating at a higher level of commitment and spirituality than was originally asked for and promised?
(See '7 *Some Further Questions*', p 124)

(d) Would a 'sabbatical' year from time to time be a good procedure – *ie* a year in which elders, in rotation, get a break from their normal duties, a year in which they would undertake some kind of training or research?

Training (pp 59-61)

• As a Session, how do you go about developing:

(a) your spirituality and understanding of the faith?
(b) your ability as individuals to talk about your faith?
(c) your pastoral skills?
(d) your understanding of the overall work of your congregation?
(e) your grasp of local issues and needs?
(f) and of wider national and international considerations?
(g) your management skills?

Consider the model regarding in-service training on page 61.

Individually, consider the areas in which you need/would welcome training.

Consider together how you could develop an on-going training programme which would enable your needs to be met.

Would it be of value to appoint a group to be responsible for this?
What financial provisions should be made for this?

Mutual support and understanding (pp 62-64)

• If you have been working your way as a Session through this chapter you will have had the opportunity to share not only your opinions, but also something of your experience and your feelings.

Have you found the opportunity of value?
If so, in what ways and why?
Has the use of small groups helped you to reach levels 3, 2 or 1 in John Powell's 'Communication Levels' on page 62?
At what level does your Session usually operate?
Is the use of small groups and the opportunity to share feelings part of the life of your Session?
If not, why not?

If not, should it be?
If it should be, how could you help it to happen?
If not already done, consider how you could arrange for the pastoral support of each other, and of each other's families, including the minister and his/her family?

Consider the model on page 63.

Page 87 indicates the importance of the minister's role in the support of the elder.

The Session clerk can also play a vital role in this regard.

The district team provides enormous support as the team members cover for each other and for each other's families.

The full Session team is yet another line of support.
Formulate recommendations for your Session regarding how you might increase your mutual support.

Bring groups together to share their findings and recommendations.

Time together (page 64)

- It takes real commitment of time to:
- fulfil the leadership goals of a modern Session;
- build Session teamwork;
- develop effective management.

- Consider as individuals:
Do you take part in Sunday worship:
- most Sundays?   YES/NO
- more or less
only when on duty?   YES/NO
- infrequently?   YES/NO

How many Session meetings have you attended ....
been unable to attend ....
chosen not to attend ....
in the past year?

List other congregational activities you take part in each week.
....
....
....

How many hours do you devote in a typical month
to your pastoral work? ....
to a specialist role? ....
(*eg* Session clerk, industrial elder)

Do you feel you give
enough time ....
too little time ....
too much time ....
to your work as an elder?

Note any changes you would wish to make regarding any of the above.

What do you feel about belonging to your Session team?

Share in small groups, what you feel free to share regarding the questions in this section.

We are
Stewards

of the Gospel.

- Talk together about the amount of time your Session has spent together in the past year.

– number of
business meetings ....
– total in hours ....
Was this enough?   YES/NO

– number of conferences/
training meetings ....
– total in hours ....
Was this enough?   YES/NO

– number of opportunities to relax and have fun together ....
– total in hours ....
Was this enough?   YES/NO

Are there any changes you would wish to recommend as a result of your discussions to help you become more of a team and the 'team of the teams'?

- In small groups:
Consider how you might develop your individual and spiritual life and how you might do this together.

5 *Team management* (pp 67-97)

- The following Bible studies could form a series of half-hour study periods on the agenda of three consecutive Session meetings. Or they could be tackled by three different groups during a time of conference.

(a) The New Testament describes a Christian congregation as 'The Body of Christ'.
Consider: 1 Corinthians 12:12-27
1 Corinthians 10:16-17
Romans 12:4-8
Ephesians 4:16
What does the term 'The Body of Christ' mean to you?
What does it say to you about teamwork, participation, management?

(b) Study Jesus' parables of 'The Shrewd Manager' (Luke 16:1-12) and 'The Talents' (Matthew 25:14-30).
What do they say to you about the qualities of a Christian in the area of management?

(c) Consider the following texts on Christian stewardship:
1 Corinthians 4:1-2
1 Peter 4:8-11.
What do they say about Christian stewardship in your Session?

Leadership and motivation (p 70-71)

• Together the minister and clerk could consider:
their relationship to each other;
how they lead the business of the Session;
if they enable or tend to dominate Session?
the problems they face in being 'the team of the team of the team'.

• Without the involvement of the minister and clerk, the Session, in small groups, could consider the quotation on page 69.
Are the two principles mentioned being done in your Session? If not, why not?
In full Session consider these two principles. The minister and clerk could share the results of their conversation.

• In small groups consider what is said about: affection; rewards; involvement; and control – and how they operate in your Session.

• Arrange to meet as a Session to consider how you might increase participation.

By way of preparation, have each other consider the ideas outlined on page 71, for example:

your present structures;
the use of small groups;
access to the agenda;
allocation of tasks;
rotation of duties;
formal and informal meetings;
seating arrangements.

In small groups, consider recommendations you would make.
Share your recommendations and consider how you might implement them.

A group might be established to aid the carrying out of any recommendations agreed by Session.

Structures (pp 75-78)

• In small groups:
If you do not operate working parties, consider what is said regarding the value of working parties.

Discuss the Management Model on page 74.
What do you like about it?
What do you dislike?
Make recommendations regarding the creation of working parties and what tasks they might be given.
Share findings.

NB In small Sessions, and large Sessions, the help of non-Session members could/should be engaged.

- In small groups:
  If you already operate working parties, consider the guidelines 1-8 on pp 76-77.
  Consider also your pattern of working parties in the light of the leadership goals outlined in chapter 2. Formulate any recommendations you would wish to put to Session. Share findings.

- Consider what is said regarding the structure of time on pp 77-78.

Personnel planning (pp 78-80)

- Consider the four sub-headings in this section and prepare recommendations.
  Where Session numbers permit, the Session could be divided into three groups, with elders free to choose a topic of interest.

(a) *Rota and time limits and talent spotting*
  Make a list of the talents needed in your congregation.
  Make a list of the jobs available in the life of your congregation.

(b) *In-service training*
  What's on offer?
  What could be made available?
  How could an in-service programme be implemented and by whom?

(c) *Specialist roles*
  How many do you operate?
  Consider the relationship of these 'specialists' to district work and the way you elect elders.

Decision-making (pp 81-83)

- In small groups:
  Consider how your Session meetings incorporate, or otherwise, the various issues raised in the Agenda points 1-7.
  Look together at the section entitled 'Control and delegation' (p 83). Formulate any recommendations the groups would wish to put to the full Session.
  Share comments/recommendations.

Communications (pp 85-86)

- Establish three working parties to research your present means of communication:
  1 within the Session;
  2 within the congregation;
  3 beyond the congregation
  – and how you might improve your lines of communication.
  Share your findings and ideas.

Assessment (pp 88-91)

- Establish two working parties each to tackle one of the following:
(a) The questions on page 89.
(b) To carry out the assessment exercise on page 90.

  Each working party should prepare a written report for issue to all the members of the Session prior to

discussion of their findings.
Pinpoint the lessons to be learned.
Consider courses of action these lessons point you towards.
Consider the possibility of creating a review group to aid continuous monitoring of the effectiveness of the Session's structures and achievement level.

• If not already done so, establish the means to assess your Session's performance regarding the leadership goals outlined in chapter 2.

The effective team (pp 91, 94-95)

• Consider what is said on page 94. In small groups have everyone share what they believe and feel about the following questions:

Forward planning
Where does God want us now to go?

Priorities
What is important to establishing God's Kingdom in our Session and congregation?

Policies
For example:
    Youth policy; Session teamwork
    Ministry of congregation
What is it that God wants us to do regarding our priorities?

Strategies
For example:
    Pastoral work; Evangelism
What course of action does God require us to take to effect our policies?

These questions should be taken separately with the groups' answers charted and God's direction sought for each in turn.

In this way your Session will together write its future agenda.

6 *Gaining ground* (pp 98-105)

• As a Session consider the illness to health analogy.
Are there any lessons to be learned from it for your Session?
• Consider the diagram on page 99. Are there lessons to be learned from it for your Session.
• Study together the Bible references on page 105.

7 *Some further questions*

– Would you like to be released from your vows?   YES/NO
– Would you wish some opportunity to discuss whether to continue or to seek release?   YES/NO
– Do you wish to continue to serve as an elder?   YES/NO
– Would you welcome an active sabbatical period?   YES/NO
– In what areas would you wish further training? ....
– If invited to become an elder are you prepared to consider the possibility seriously?   YES/NO
– If yes, what help would you require?
....

APPENDIX 1
A Care Visiting Scheme

To set out to involve others in pastoral care requires careful planning.

There should be *preparation* for those who take part, helping them to work out what they are expected to do.

Good communication is needed between lay-carers and the minister, between lay-carers and the elders.

A system should be set up so that every person involved *knows their role*. As part of this, lines of responsibility and accountability are required, which means people must know who reports to whom and how confidentiality is to be maintained. Some outside reference point is helpful, a person or small group that can act as advisors regarding such a scheme.

With these basic principles, individual congregations may develop very different patterns relevant to their own situation and the skills and experience of the people participating.

An example

Here is a real example from a large suburban parish. This parish sought to provide better care for their housebound elderly, those with chronic illnesses, people with learning difficulties, and some of those struggling with bereavement.

The scheme was initially set up when there was a full-time lay worker with a social work background. The lay-worker co-ordinated the scheme and then handed over this co-ordinating role to a member of

the congregation who had trained in counselling at Simpson House.

Originally two groups of 10-12 women came to three preparation evenings and then were given one or two people to visit.

Over the past 5 years two more groups have been established. The training of the lay visitors continues in one or two training evenings each year. There is a regular support structure which all visitors are expected to attend. They meet every three months in the groups in which they trained. In these support meetings each visitors takes a turn to share their experience of visiting, their enjoyment of it and any problems they are finding. In this way they are supported in their task, learn from each other, and experience a strong sense of fellowship.

The role of the lay visitor could be described as providing 'a ministry of supportive friendship' to people who are isolated and unable to take part in church services and other church activities. The caring presence of the church goes out to them where they are, through the lay visitor. The role is seen as primarily one of 'being with' people rather than an active 'doing' role.

Several people made this scheme possible. Initially the minister's role was vital: he took the initiative and was highly involved in the planning of the structure, the training and the group meetings. Over time his involvement has lessened, or become more of a 'back seat' role.

The co-ordinator's role is a crucial one. Her time commitment averages about ten hours a week. She liaises with the minister; makes initial visits to assess new people to be visited; makes the first visit to introduce the visitor; sees lay visitors individually to monitor the work, especially initially; and is involved with the necessary administration.

The elders have been always informed of developments, both at the inception of the scheme and if there is to be a lay visitor used in their district. At first, for some, the scheme was perceived as a threat, but over time its value has been more appreciated and elders are among those who now refer people for a lay visitor. Local doctors and social workers also occasionally suggest people for visiting. The scheme is not restricted to church members.

There is an advisory group consisting of two elders, a lay visitor, minister, co-ordinator, and out-side consultant. This met every six months at the beginning and now meetings are only called when necessary.

APPENDIX 2
For members of a small Session

A suggestion for management

It has been said, 'Only do separately what you cannot do together'.

In one linked charge, it has proved helpful for the four Kirk Sessions to meet together as one on a bi-monthly basis. This meeting is called the 'General Kirk Session' and has its own clerk and treasurer. Each individual Kirk Session – after discussion – formally agreed to hand over to the General Kirk Session (GKS) all matters of common interest.

A Steering Group, consisting of all the Session clerks and treasurers, along with the minister, meets prior to each meeting of the GKS to formulate the agenda.

At each meeting of the GKS the first hour is given over to discussion of a special subject. These are sometimes matters passed down by the General Assembly or Presbytery, but they are always of wide general Church importance. The Steering Group chooses them and arranges for their presentation by an outside speaker with some expertise, or by a small group of the members. (Recent examples include Revd John Harvey on the Iona Community; and a group with financial expertise on the national Church financial crisis and how it affects us). In all cases, elders are encouraged to explore issues and take action where appropriate.

The rest of the meeting is taken up with discussion of matters held to be in common: for example Christian Aid; an approach to young people, a missionary partner, the joint parish magazine, the Presbytery, joint finance and property, *etc.* A further hour should cover these.

Matters concerning individual Kirk Sessions may occasionally require separate meetings, though much can be dealt with at the kirk before or after the Morning Service. Often things can be attended to by the Session Clerk on an informal basis.

For smaller Kirk Sessions, where they are not involved in an official linking, joint meetings with neighbouring kirks could have the value of increasing opportunities for elders to become better informed, of sharing ideas and insights, and of taking joint action where possible.

APPENDIX 3
Contacts and Acknowledgements

Contacts

For information about resources/training opportunities in UK Presbyterian Denominations contact:

Church of Scotland
Board of Parish Education
St Colm's Centre, 20 Inverleith Terrace
Edinburgh EH3 5NS
Tel: 0131-332-0343

Presbyterian Church in Ireland
Director of Christian Training
Christian Training Centre
Magee House, 7 Rugby Road
Belfast BT7 1PS
Tel: 01232-248424

Presbyterian Church of Wales:
Coleg Trefeca
Trefeca
Talgarth
Nr Brecon
Powys LD3 0PP
Tel: 01874-711423

United Reformed Church:
86 Tavistock Place
London WC1H 9RT
Tel: 0171-916-2020

Acknowledgements

The Publishers wish to acknowledge the following individuals and organisations for their kind permission to reproduce illustrations and copyright material in this book:

Authors – photographs on p iv, v; Board of Parish Education, Church of Scotland – *Frontline* material; David Simon - illustration work; Graeme Leonard for editorial and layout work on original edition; Lesley A Taylor – setting of this edition and general illustration work; John McWilliam – illustrations on pp vii, 111 (*bottom*).

General thanks are also due to:

Ronald Barclay	Graeme Brown
Dorothy Dalgleish	Rowland Dalgleish
Jenny Garrard	David Henry
James Hewer	Andrew McLellan
Jean Morrison	Terry Oakley
Jean Steele	

The illustrative cover shot on this book was taken by Paul Turner. It is of Craiglockhart Parish Church, Edinburgh and its surrounding area.

'Session Matters' articles, written by Stewart Matthew, have been reprinted with the kind permission of the editor of *Life and Work*, the Church of Scotland's magazine, in which they first appeared.

Thanks are due to Sheilah Steven, National Adviser in Elder Training, for encouraging the revision of this work, and to all others who, either directly or indirectly, have contributed to it.

Also available from Saint Andrew Press: *Leading God's People* (companion volume) by Stewart Matthew and Kenneth Scott and *Session Matters* by Stewart Matthew.

NOTES

NOTES

NOTES

NOTES

NOTES